The Young Adult's Guide to Financial Success

How to
Manage Your Money,
Live Better on Less,
Be Debt Free,
Invest Wisely, and
Prepare For Retirement

Edward M. Wolpert

Oconee Financial Planning Services LLC

Published by Oconee Financial Planning Services LLC www.oconeefps.com

This book is intended to provide authoritative and useful information. It represents the opinions and ideas of the author and is in no way a blanket recommendation for all persons in all situations. Further, nothing contained herein is meant to be construed as financial or tax advice. The author and publisher hereby specifically disclaim any responsibility for any possible liability, loss, risk, personal or otherwise, which might be incurred as a consequence, whether directly or indirectly, of the use and/or application of any of the content of this book.

Cover design by Cheryl Klinginsmith

ISBN 978-0-9800769-2-9

Printed in the United States of America

SAUL WOLPERT (1905—1994)

WILL ROBERTS (1924—   )

Dedicated to my father and my father-in-law.
Their lives embody the principles of this book.
It is written for the millions of twenty, thirty, and
forty year olds who desire financial success.

CONTENTS

CHAPTER ONE
INTRODUCTION

I am a lucky man. In the younger generations of my family, I have wonderful children, grandchildren, stepchildren, children-in-law, and many nieces and nephews. Most of them are in their 20s and 30s, with a few still teenagers and a few who have hit the big 40. Some are married and some are not, but they all need to know the information provided In this book. This book is written for them and others like them. Why?

I had a conversation with a niece of mine a while back. She is newly married with a small child, and she and her husband have gotten themselves behind the eight ball, financially speaking. Presently, their income is not great, and they have incurred debt that they can't handle. They went to a workshop aimed at improving their financial position, and they have taken its message to heart. They have reformed some bad habits, and are making strides toward financial stability.

It struck me: How did they get into that situation to begin with? What did they know, or not know, about money and debt? Could their situation have been avoided altogether? As I recalled the conversation, the answer became clear. They simply didn't know how to handle money. They didn't have a budget. They couldn't track their income and expenses. Their finances were out of control, and it all could have been avoided with some knowledge and discipline. Presently, they are on their way to financial stability, and for that I am grateful.

But there is more that they need to know to have a financially successful household. If they were to know it, their chance for financial success would be greatly improved. That's when I decided to write a book for them and others like them.

How Much Do You Know About Money?

In the United States of America, the wealthiest nation in the history of the world, it is possible to be educated through the postgraduate college level, and in all that time, no one ever taught you the facts of financial life. No one taught you about MONEY.

You can have all that education, and somehow never have taken a course in economics, much less a course in personal finance. Economics is the study of the production, consumption, and transfer of money, or wealth. Personal finance is the application of economics to individuals or members of a household. Perhaps you know about neither.

> **Personal Finance is...**
> The application of economics to your household.

It's possible that no one ever taught you about:
- how to budget your income and expenses
- the difference between a stock and a bond
- the cost of debt, and how you have to pay it back
- how time can be a more important factor in compounding savings than the amount of money saved
- compound interest, and the magic of the number 72

Are You Serious?

If you are reading this book, I hope you are serious about getting your financial life in order. Many young adults don't think much about their financial life. Often, they engage in behaviors that get them in financial trouble very quickly. Other young adults try to get their financial lives in order, but they start late, and have severe handicaps to overcome before things get better.

I'm sure that in your younger years, while growing up, you thought about what your life would be like. You probably had plans and dreams as you contemplated the future. If you're like most people, what you want out of life is love, professional success, security, and happiness. Money has something to do with the last three.

You need to know about personal finance since it will influence so much of your life.

Personal Finance and Life

Everything in life has an economic aspect to it. And most decisions in life involve trade-offs, each of which has a financial impact. Yet, as a society, we have not provided our citizens--especially our younger generations--with the information they need to make a financial go of their lives. The omission of financial education is a disgrace of major proportions, and is a serious impediment to anyone's success in life.

Many young adults go out on their own, setting up their households after graduating from high school or college, and have no idea what they are doing financially. They lack financial savvy, and are easy prey for those elements of our society that can profit from their ignorance.

The Poverty Industry

In August 2008, a Bill Moyers Journal presentation was aired on Public Television. It was entitled, "The Poverty Industry." It showed how millions of young adults (and older ones, too) get into debt, and how they sink deeper and deeper into it. What a depressing situation!

There are those among us (Moyers calls it an "industry") who capitalize on the financial ignorance of everyday people, basically decent individuals who are very trusting and just don't understand what they are doing. They don't read the fine print of agreements they sign. They don't understand the concept of collateral-securing debt (e.g. car debt), which, if not paid, subjects the collateral to forfeiture. They are easily misled, and end up poorer than they might otherwise have been. In most cases, some basic personal finance education could have helped them escape the cycle of ongoing poverty. This book seeks to remedy that problem.

3

What is "Financial Success?"

The title of this book contains the words "financial success." At first thought, financial success might be defined as any, or all, of the following:

- having plenty of money
- buying whatever you want
- living in a big house
- driving a luxury car
- having an extensive wardrobe
- traveling wherever you want to
- quitting your job and retiring early

For many people, these are desirable activities, and certainly, if you have a lot of money you can do these things. But I define financial success somewhat differently. To me, financial success is:

- living a reasonably secure and comfortable life, considering the amount of money you earn
- having a state of mind in which you feel free, independent and self-confident regarding your personal finances
- being able to pay for what you need and want, and (with a few exceptions) not need to borrow money from anyone
- being financially literate and being able to make good decisions about money
- feeling empowered by being debt-free
- having sufficient funds for an enjoyable retirement
- being personally responsible for your financial success

If you earn $250,000 a year, but spend $300,000 a year and acquire a good deal of debt, you are not financially successful. On the other hand, if you earn $75,000 a year, pay your bills, have no debt, live your life without financial stress, and have money left over at the end of each month to do with whatever you want, to my way of thinking, you are a financial success.

In other words, it's not a question of how much you earn, but rather a question of what you do with what you earn, and whether you have a life that you can enjoy. The objective of this book is to provide you with information that will enable you to be a financial success as defined above.

Who Am I to Write This Book?

There are two reasons. The first is biographical.

I was born in the middle of the Great Depression, when there was 25% unemployment and most people had little to call their own. My dad was a teacher, so we had decent and steady income, unlike many people at that time. Later, during World War II, there was rationing of many food items and consumer goods. People who had little during the Depression didn't have very much more during the War. After the War, there were consumer goods available and fuller employment, but inflation was rampant and the salary of a teacher (who had three boys and a wife to feed) didn't go very far. Add to this the fact that my parents were the children of eastern European immigrants, and you can get a picture of our very basic life as a family, in terms of material things, during my early years and teens. Like many other Americans, we weren't poor, but we just didn't have much. So, I was brought up to be careful how I spent money. Thrift, buying well, not wasting — these values were instilled from a very early age.

The second reason for this book has to do with my education and experience. I am a financial planner. I work with people to assist them in making decisions about financial matters. My clients include young and older adults. Moreover, I am a private investor with over fifty years of experience.

Many of the suggestions made in this book are the result of my education, my upbringing, and the historical and financial context in which it occurred. In other words, I've lived many of these ideas, and I can write from experience. I want to share this information so young adults can learn from my experiences instead of the often-costly trial and error method.

Is This Book for You?

This book is aimed at young adults, couples or single people, who constitute an economic unit, a household. The only characteristics I have in mind for my readers is that they are young, in their 20s or 30s, getting started with their independent adult lives, and have a desire to be financially successful.

You will find this book valuable if you:
- have limited income
- are just starting out on your own
- are a student
- are recently married
- do not want to be reliant on someone else to have money

If you fit any of these categories, then read on. If not, and you know of someone who does, then pass the book along.

The Present vs. The Future

Young adults are faced with a fundamental dilemma. They want to have a secure financial future, but they have a present life to live, which requires that they spend some of the money they earn. So, what should they do?

One approach is to deny themselves all the good things in life that require the expenditure of money. In this way, they invest everything for a secure financial future. Their present life may not be much fun, though.

On the other hand, they might decide to live only for today, spending everything they earn and then some. Live lavishly. Go on expensive vacations, dine out frequently, buy a new car every year, etc. In this way, their future life may not be much fun.

Solving the Dilemma
These two divergent viewpoints must be reconciled.

I have known people at both extremes of this present-to-future continuum and I don't recommend either position. Since no one can reliably predict the future, a prudent approach is to take care of present needs and also plan for the future.

My recommendation is to pay yourself now, and pay yourself later. Every month when you are paying your present bills, pay your future bills by investing for the future. Even households with very low income can put a little money aside to invest for future use. If you have difficulty in setting aside these funds for the future, the trick may be to not get all the money in your hands. Have an automatic deduction taken from your paycheck and sent to the investment vehicle of your choice.

Learn, Learn, Learn
You have to educate yourself about personal finance. Reading this book is a start. But from here, you need to read periodicals that deal with personal finance, such as *Money* magazine, *Smart Money*, *Kiplinger Personal Finance*, and similar materials. Like any other field in which you have received a basic education, personal finance requires systematic updating, so you can be assured that you are current in your knowledge of the subject.

Setting Financial Goals
Goal setting is a key element in achieving financial success. There are three issues you have to confront:

1. Goals should be long-term and short-term.

You need to identify what your goals are. This will vary from person to person. Most people have a goal of being able to afford a comfortable retirement. For you, this is probably a long-term goal, maybe forty or fifty years away. On the other hand, having enough money to put a down payment on a house is much closer to the present, perhaps five or ten years away. Both need to be planned for.

2. Goals should be specific.

Having a goal of being able to afford a comfortable retirement is a worthy one. But you need to put a dollar amount on that idea. In today's dollars, how much money would you need to have to meet this goal? $50,000 annually? $80,000 annually? The same thinking should go into the idea of a down payment on a house. Will you need $20,000? Or $40,000? Having a dollar amount will give you a target.

3. Goals should be realistic.

Most people would like to have several million dollars when they retire. But if your anticipated income will be modest, this may be unattainable. So, looking at your income, expenses, life style, etc. what would be a reasonable goal?

More information about setting personal finance goals can be found at **www.aboutgoal-setting.com**.

> **Your Goals**
>
> Should be specific, realistic, and have a time frame.

The Phases of Your Financial Life

Your approach to personal finance will vary with where you are in your life. Generally, there are three identifiable phases:

1. Accumulation – This occurs in your early earning years, from approximately 25 to 55 years of age. Here is where you start your career, and hopefully advance to the point where you are continuously increasing your income. You are accumulating wealth. Most readers of this book will be in this phase.

2. Accumulation and preservation – This phase lasts from age 55 to your retirement. Here, you continue to accumulate wealth,

but your investments will need to be somewhat more conservative. This is because if some of your more volatile investments go sour, you probably won't have enough time to set them right.

3. Distribution – This generally begins when you retire. The wealth that you've accumulated over your lifetime will be distributed to yourself to partially fund your retirement. The remainder of your wealth can be distributed to others — family or charities — as you desire.

Your Household is Your Business

The key concept in achieving financial success is to consider your household, yourself and those who live with you under the same roof, as a small business. A business sells goods or services that produce revenues. Then it pays its expenses, and what's left over is profit. Its owners may use the profit for whatever purposes they want.

Similarly, as a household, you produce income from salaries, fees, or other sources, and from these sources, you pay your household expenses. What remains after the bills are paid is your discretionary income, to spend or invest as you see fit.

Income - Expenses = Discretionary Cash

Obviously, businesses must make a profit to stay alive. Sometimes they incur debt as part of their financial plans. Servicing this debt, paying back the loan plus the interest charged, is an important expense that must be taken care of in a timely manner. If the debt is not paid back, for whatever reason, a business may go bankrupt and cease to exist. Alternatively, it may reorganize and re-enter its industry as a more viable business entity in a stronger financial position.

Your household works the same way, except that if you go bankrupt, you may not ever be able to obtain credit. If you can, you will be paying a very high interest rate. Your future will be severely impaired.

Simple as it sounds, the most important rule in achieving financial success is to ensure that your income exceeds your expenses. As business journalist Charles A. Jaffe puts it, "It's not your salary that makes you rich, it's your spending habits." In later chapters, you will learn many strategies for spending your money effectively.

Take the Emotion Out of Your Finances

Our emotions make us human. A life without emotions is a life too dull to even contemplate. But when it comes to money, put your emotions aside. Emotions are often temporary and fleeting. Your financial goals, however, are long-term, and when your emotions abate, progress on your financial goals may be severely impaired. All the planning and discipline could end up being wasted. So, make your decisions on a purely rational, self-controlled basis. This is the way to financial success. Save the emotions for your personal life, not your finances.

A Word for Couples

Relationships can be difficult under the best of circumstances. When most couples have difficulties, more often than not, the problems involve sex or money. This book will focus on money. However, it should be recognized that money problems could interfere with many aspects of a relationship, including sex. In other words, problems with the checkbook can easily find themselves relocating to the bedroom.

Accordingly, I suggest some ground rules for couples, and if they are followed, the chances for financial success are enhanced. If they are not, it is going to be much more difficult.

We're Both In This Together

The two of you need to agree on a financial strategy. You should be in this together, as one economic unit. If one person follows the strategy and the other doesn't, resentment will follow and your relationship will suffer.

> ### Remember
> Couples need to agree on financial matters.

In Money Matters, Are We the Same or Different?

Some people are savers, and some are spenders. If one of you is a saver and the other is a spender, you have to agree to both sign on to your strategy as a household, and be honest with yourselves. If you are both savers, your life will be easier. If you are both spenders, you will have to discipline yourselves to be financially successful.

Keeping Track of Everything

Someone has to keep the books, that is, keep track of income and expenses. Such a task is best done by one person in consultation with the other. In many instances in life, when everybody is in charge, nobody is in charge. And so it is with personal finance.

Whose Job Comes First?

If you are both working, it would be worthwhile to agree on who will be the primary breadwinner, the primary source of income. It could be either person. It could depend upon a difference in salary, or the importance each person's career to that person. This is important because sometimes an employer wants to transfer an employee to a different location. Will the two of you move to the new location? Can one of you work from your home, wherever it is? Will you have a commuter marriage? If you have determined in advance who will be the primary breadwinner, your decision is half-made.

Money: Yours, Mine, or Ours?

And finally, each person should have his or her own money. That means that regardless of who is earning how much, each person should have his or her own money, perhaps in a separate account, over which that person has absolute discretion. Then, when Person A gives to Person B a gift that costs $25, the $25 should come from Person A's money, and not from the couple' joint money. How much should each person's absolute discretionary money be? That needs to be worked out together and included in the monthly budget.

We're Ready to Begin

With our definition of financial success, our understanding of running a household like a business, and our attention to the ground rules, we are ready to get started on achieving financial success.

The ideas expressed in the following chapters are not difficult to grasp. Indeed, they are common sense, for the most part. We will see how to:

- find out your current financial status
- know where your money is coming from and where it is going
- use credit cards appropriately
- spend money wisely
- avoid wasteful practices
- use debt appropriately
- prepare for retirement
- gain and protect wealth
- prepare to buy a house

The Importance of Focus and Discipline

There is one final and important thought that needs to be expressed before we get into the details of personal finance. None of this information will do you any good unless you can develop the discipline to do what needs to be done, and to control your financial behavior.

Andrew Carnegie, super-wealthy industrialist and philanthropist of the late nineteenth and early twentieth centuries, was once asked what was the key to his success. He gave a very simple answer: Every morning, make a list of things you need to do that day. Then, do them.

He didn't say to do the easy things, the fun things, or the things that make you happy. He said to do the things that need to be done. Carnegie's discipline and focus was, to a large extent, what made him the success he was.

How Do I get Focus and Discipline

Some people seek help from a partner, a confidant, or someone acting in a fiduciary capacity to oversee their activities. Other people, with strong religious convictions, draw upon their faith for help. And still others just will it through sheer determination. Many people use a combination of these approaches.

Regardless of the source, focus and discipline are necessary. You use your head, your heart and your guts to stay focused on your goals. No book can teach this. It must be developed within oaoh individual person.

This book is organized in a logical progression of information, each chapter building on the preceding ones. To get the most from this book, the chapters should be read in order of presentation, with the exception of Chapter Eleven, which can be read independently.

With this in mind, let's get going!

CHAPTER TWO
WHAT ARE YOU WORTH?

Before making any plans or analyzing anything, you need to know your present financial situation. In other words, right now, what are you worth?

Businesses do this using a statement called a balance sheet. It shows, at a given time, the firm's assets (what they own), their liabilities (what they owe), and the difference between the assets and liabilities, referred to as net worth, or book value. The arithmetic is easy:

Assets – Liabilities = Net Worth

For you personally, we can restate the formula so it reads:

What you own – What you owe = What you're worth

Net Worth Statement
Households can use a statement similar to a balance sheet and call it a Net Worth Statement. In it, you list your assets and liabilities, then subtract one from another to come up with your net worth. You can classify the assets and liabilities with regard to their function and type.

When you look at your Net Worth Statement, it can tell you one of two possible things about your overall financial position. Your net worth can be:
- Positive – You have more assets than liabilities.
- Negative – Your liabilities exceed your assets. In other words, you're in debt.

Remember: Your Net Worth Statement shows your financial situation.

Valuing Your Assets

In the examples shown below in Figures 2-1 and 2-2, notice that there are two categories of assets: financial assets, and use assets. The values for the financial assets can be taken from the last statement of the institutions that hold them. The same holds true for the liabilities.

The values for the use assets should be your estimate of their market value, which is what a perfect stranger might pay for them at an auction.

Figure 2-1
Nancy Miller
Net Worth Statement
December 18, 2008

ASSETS		
Financial Assets		
Checking Account	$936	
Savings Account	2,752	
Money Market Account	3,378	
IRA	3,451	
401(k)	11,263	
Total Financial Assets		$21,780
Use Assets		
Furniture/Household Goods	$3,500	
Vehicle	5,500	
Jewelry	1,500	
Total Use Assets		$10,500
TOTAL ASSETS		**$32,280**
LIABILITIES		
Credit Cards	$1,872	
Student Loans	5,831	
TOTAL LIABILITIES		**$7,703**
NET WORTH		**$24,577**

Example of a Good Statement
Figure 2-1 is an example of a Net Worth Statement for a fictional young woman, Nancy Miller. She is in her late 20s, employed at a job she loves, and rents an apartment.

Nancy has a net worth of $24,577, pretty good for her age. She has $7,086 in cash in her checking, savings, and money market accounts, which is nice, but really should be higher in case of a sudden need. Her vehicle is valued at $5,500, meaning it is several years old and has been fairly well depreciated already. Her liabilities are few, and not excessive. She pays off her credit card debt balance every month, and continues to pay off her student loans. Nancy is in decent financial shape. Her net worth is positive $24,577. She owns more than she owes. She has a good start to financial success.

Example of a Poor Statement
Now look at Figure 2-2, the Net Worth Statement of Lisa and Morgan Silverod. This couple is in their mid 30s, own their house, and both work outside the home.

You would think that with both of them pulling in decent salaries, their financial situation would be good. In total, they have assets totaling $491,494. They seem to be living the good life. They own their house, drive fairly new cars, and have an RV and a boat.

But look at all that debt!

Too Much Debt
Not only is their house mortgaged to the hilt, with $350,00 of debt (first and second mortgages) on a house valued at $370,000, but they also have large amounts of credit card debt, as well as car, RV, and boat loans. As a result of this debt, they have a net worth of negative $1,553. They are not in good financial shape. Also, they don't have very much cash or equivalents on hand to survive a financial emergency – only $1,278 in checking and $3,338 in savings, totaling $4,616.

Figure 2-2
Lisa and Morgan Silverod
Net Worth Statement
December 27, 2008

ASSETS		
Financial Assets		
Checking Account	$1,278	
Savings Account	3,338	
401(k), Lisa	12,927	
401(k), Morgan	16,451	
Total Financial Assets		$33,994
Use Assets		
Residence	$370,000	
RV	13,000	
Boat	20,500	
Furniture/Household Goods	7,500	
Vehicle, Lisa	22,500	
Vehicle, Morgan	19,500	
Jewelry	4,500	
Total Use Assets		$457,500
TOTAL ASSETS		**$491,494**
LIABILITIES		
Mortage Loan	$329,420	
Second Mortgage Loan	20,580	
RV Loan	13,750	
Boat Loan	15,000	
Credit Card, Lisa	47,720	
Credit Card, Morgan	32,561	
Car Loan #1	18,588	
Car Loan #2	15,428	
TOTAL LIABILITIES		**$493,047**
NET WORTH		**($1,553)**

Construct Your Own Net Worth Statement

Using these two Net Worth Statements as examples, do one for your household. Use a simple Excel spreadsheet, or do it with pencil and paper.

If your net worth is positive like Nancy's, you have a good beginning toward financial success. This book will tell you how to increase your net worth.

If your net worth is negative like Lisa and Morgan's, you are starting from behind, but with some discipline, you can achieve a positive net worth and be on the road to financial success. You will first need to get out of debt to get to square one. Then, you'll need to stay out of debt to build positive cash flow.

Developing a Net Worth Statement is the first step in dealing with your finances. It tells you your net worth at that moment in time. However, as we look toward the future, we'll need to see how much money is coming into the household, and how much is going out. This leads us to the next chapter, Money In/Money Out.

CHAPTER 3
MONEY IN/MONEY OUT

In the last chapter, we developed a Net Worth Statement to give us an idea of what you're worth at the time of that statement. That's a necessary analysis to get us started. Now, we look at a more dynamic aspect of your finances: your income and expenses. We want to see how much money is coming into the household, and how much is going out. This analysis is called a cash flow analysis, and gives us an opportunity to track income and expenditures. This is a little more difficult than discovering your net worth, as we shall soon see. But it's time well spent. You need to know this information in order to be able to control your financial life.

Your Household Is Your Business
As mentioned in Chapter One, your household is like a small business. Money comes in through your income and money goes out to cover expenses. Every business seeks to increase income as much as possible, and keep expenses down as much as possible. The result will be an increase in profit. You will need to do the same thing, but in your case, the difference between your income and expenses will be your discretionary income that will allow you to pay down debt (if any), build wealth, and fulfill your financial goals.

Cash Flow Statement
The analysis of your income and expenses will result in a Cash Flow Statement. The format for this statement is a simple one:

- List income by source. How much cash is coming in and from where?
- List expenses by function. How much cash is going out, and to whom or for what?

- Subtract the expenses from the income, and the result is your cash flow.

This statement should be done for a year, usually the last full calendar year. In other words, last year how much money came in, and where did it go? To develop your first Cash Flow Statement will require some time and effort. But in subsequent years, the format will already have been set up, and modifications will involve merely making adjustments to the previous year's statement.

> **Your Cash Flow Statement**
>
> Shows the money coming in, and where it's going.

Income and Expenses

Here are some of the items needed for a Cash Flow Statement. You'll notice that virtually all of the possible sources of income and types of expenditures are listed. I don't expect that you'll use even half of them. But they are listed so you don't forget anything. Try to be as complete as you can.

Income

This should be fairly easy to do. List the sources and amounts. The salary amount should be the gross amount, which is your actual salary, not your take home pay. This can be readily ascertained by examining your pay statement. Don't include any one time/non-recurring money received, such as an inheritance or a gift. Income items include salaries, fees, tips, self-employment income, dividends, capital gains, trust income, alimony received, child support received, and any other income (specify).

Expenses

This is a much longer list, since you will probably have many more expenses than sources of income. I don't expect you to use all these items. Select those that are applicable to your household. Provide the information with as much accuracy as possible.

To save some time in estimating recurring items with payments that may differ from month to month, such as utilities, total the payments made in three typical months such as February, June and October, then multiply that total by four. Then enter that amount in your analysis. Sometimes estimates will have to be made. That's fine. Just be as accurate as you can.

Don't Double Count

Be careful when you categorize expenses that you don't duplicate or overlap. For example, you might use your credit card to purchase clothing items, or vacation-specific expenses such as airline tickets. Those expenses should be categorized as clothing, or vacations, respectively. The only credit card expense occurs only when you don't pay off the monthly balance, and you have to pay interest.

Itemize each source of income and each category of expense. Add up your income, subtract your expenses, and the result should be your net cash flow, which is your discretionary cash.

Nancy's Cash Flow Statement

Do you remember Nancy Miller from the last chapter? She had a net worth of $24,597. Figure 3-1 is an example of Nancy's Cash Flow Statement for the calendar year 2008.

Expense Items:
alimony paid
cable/satellite TV
car fuel
car insurance
car loan payments
car repairs/
    maintenance savings
cell phone
child support
clothing
credit card interest
dining out
electricity
entertainment
federal income taxes
FICA/Medicare
    retirement plans
food
health insurance
house insurance
house maintenance
gas
gifts (charitable)
gifts (non-charitable)
mortgage loan payment
    (principal and
    interest)
medical/dental
    expenses
new investments
    education
paid professional
    expenses
    (accounting, legal,
    etc.)
property tax
personal care
rent
state income taxes
student loan payments
telephone
vacations
veterinary expenses
water/sewage
other expenses (specify)

Figure 3-1
Nancy Miller's Statement of Cash Flows, 2008

CASH OUT		CASH IN	
		Salary	$76,000
		Interest	280
CASH OUT		**TOTAL CASH IN**	**$76,280**
401(k)		$1,868	
Apartment Insurance		280	
Cable TV/Internet		1,800	
Car Fuel and Maintenance		2,856	
Car Insurance		2,046	
Cell Phone		1,100	
Chartitable Contributions		4,200	
Cleaners		400	
Clothes		4,720	
Dental Insurance		283	
Electricity		398	
Entertainment/Dining Out		1,900	
Federal Witholding		12,920	
FICA/Medicare		5,814	
Food		2,780	
Gas (House)		580	
Gifts		500	
IRA		1,500	
LT Disability Insurance		76	
Medical Insurance		883	
Phone (Land line)		452	
Pocket Money		2,200	
Rent		10,320	
State Withholding		1,115	
Student Loan Payments		1,000	
Vacation		1,500	
Veterinary Payments		200	
Water		164	
TOTAL CASH OUT		**$63,855**	
		NET CASH FLOW	**$12,425**

She Is In Great Shape

Nancy's cash flow statement looks terrific. Almost all income comes from her salary. Her net cash flow is a positive $12,425. Her expenses are not excessive. Overall, she's in excellent shape, living well within her means and planning for the future.

This statement took a bit of time for her to develop, especially accounting for all the expenses. In this case, as is the case with many households, Nancy knew what her income was, because it's received by check. And she knew what most of her expenses were, because they are paid by check or automatic bank draft. But when it comes to cash transactions, she has to guess what her expenditures are. That's because there are many expenses she might not even notice. Typically, these are small payments made in cash from her "pocket money."

Pocket Money Expenses

If you find yourself in the position of going through large amounts of pocket money and not knowing where it is going, try this: For one month, a typical month of the year, track your cash expenditures. For every outgo of cash over $1, make a note of the amount and the purpose. You'd be surprised at what you might find out at the end of the month. One client of mine realized that she was spending $4 every workday morning on a cup of gourmet coffee. Do the math: $4 times 5 workdays in the week is $20 dollars per week. In 50 weeks of work this amounted to $1,000 for the year. She hadn't even realized how much she was spending on coffee.[1]

Cigarette smokers spend a copious amount of money on their habit. A pack of cigarettes costs about $4. Again, do the math. A two-pack-a-day smoker will spend $8 per day, or $1,460 per year. Add to that the increased health problems associated with smoking and the reduced life expectancy of smokers, and this nicotine habit is expensive indeed.

---

1   In July 2008, a coffee-addicted journalist figured out that a barrel of Starbuck's latte costs about $1,200. Oil, then at $140 a barrel, seemed rather inexpensive by comparison.

Construct Your Own Cash Flow Statement

Using Nancy's Cash Flow Statement as an example, construct one for yourself. Again, use a simple Excel spreadsheet, or do it with pencil and paper if desired.

When you've done an analysis of your cash flow, the bottom line – income minus expenses – will reveal whether your cash position is positive or negative. If it is positive, congratulate yourself. You're living within your means, and perhaps you can make it even more positive. If it is negative, then you have some work to do.

Budgeting

A budget is a plan for spending. Every business has a budget for its coming year. Revenues and expenses must be anticipated, to make sure there is positive cash flow for the year. You, too, need to do this.

To develop a budget, start with your cash flow statement. Last year's income and expenditures are shown there.

> ## Remember
> You can develop your budget from your Cash Flow Statement.

Total Pay or Take-Home Pay?

If you want to simplify things, and if your income is derived from wages or salaries from which deductions are made (income tax withholding, FICA, pension contributions, etc.), use your net income, also known as your take-home pay, as the income portion of your budget. But then, of course, be sure not to include the payroll deductions in the expense portion of the budget. If you do this in the simplified form, be sure that you are aware of your employment-sponsored retirement contributions. They are an important part of your net worth and your future. They will reduce your take-home pay, but you need to keep your eye on this to ensure that you are taking full advantage of these retirement benefits and they are growing appropriately. I prefer the non-simplified way because it shows more clearly what's going on, so that version is presented below.

Now let's focus on your expenses (this includes your analysis of your small cash expenditures, such as gourmet coffee).

How Much Is Enough, and How Much Is Too Much?

Look at your Cash Flow Statement. Are there any places where you are spending money unwisely? Is your rent more than 30% of your gross income? Maybe you need a less expensive apartment. Do you need both a cell phone and a landline? Could one or the other meet your needs? Can any other expenses be reduced? Are there other expenses that you'd like to increase? Are there any expenses that might increase through no fault of yours, such as increases in electricity or food costs? If so, add 5% or so to the figure from last year's cash flow statement. This is called *positive padding*, and it gives you a margin of error.

Constructing Your Budget

Now, extend last year's Cash Flow Statement to this year's budget, making modifications as needed. Then, add up your budgeted expenses. They should be less than the income received, thus yielding a positive cash flow. If they are not, then your cash flow will be negative and you'll need to either increase your income, reduce your expenses, or both.

If your budget is to be a helpful plan, it should be realistic and flexible. Modify your budget accordingly, making adjustments as needed before you begin the year. You are aiming to start the year with a balanced budget, in which you know how much money is coming in and what you plan to do with it. Be prepared to make further modifications as the year progresses.

Nancy Miller's Budget for Next Year

Figure 3-2 is an example of Nancy's budget for 2009, derived from her 2008 Cash Flow Statement presented above. She started with her Cash Flow Statement, and added another column for the budget. This gave her an opportunity to easily compare last year's actual with this year's anticipated expenditures.

Figure 3-2
Nancy Miller

CASH IN	2008 CASH FLOW	CHANGES	2009 BUDGET
Salary	$76,000	$3,000	$79,000
Interest	280	345	625
TOTAL CASH IN	**$76,280**		**$79,625**
CASH OUT			
401(k)	$1,868	$652	$2,520
Apartment Insurance	280		280
Cable TV/Internet	1,800		1,800
Car Fuel and Maintenance	2,856		2,856
Car Insurance	2,046		2,046
Cell Phone	1,100		1,100
Chartitable Contributions	4,200	300	4,500
Cleaners	400		400
Clothes	4,720	-220	4,500
Dental Insurance	283		283
Electricity	398		398
Entertainment/Dining Out	1,900	100	2,000
Federal Withholding	12,920	600	13,520
FICA/Medicare	5,814	52	5,866
Food	2,780		2,780
Gas (House)	580		580
Gifts	500	100	600
IRA	1,500	500	2,000
Long-Term Disability Insurance	76		76
Medical Insurance	883		883
Phone (Land Line)	452		452
Pocket Money	2,200		2,200
Rainy Day/Capital Expense Fund	0	13,401	13,401
Rent	10,320		10,320
State Withholding	1,115	285	1,400
Student Loan Payments	1,000		1,000
Vacation	1,500		1,500
Veterinary Payments	200		200
Water	164		164
TOTAL CASH OUT	**$63,855**		**$79,625**
NET CASH FLOW	**$12,425**		**0**

Let's Look at Nancy's Budget

Nancy expects a $3,000 raise in her salary for 2008, and an additional $345 in interest received. She budgeted for that, and estimated what the increases would be in her income tax and payroll taxes withheld. She decided to increase her charitable giving, retirement contributions, and her gifts budget, and to spend a bit less on clothes. Her excess cash went to start her Rainy Day/Capital Expense Fund, which will be explained in Chapter Six. Her budget is balanced. Nice job.

Any small business that would start off a year with anticipated expenses greater than revenues, thus yielding no profit, might consider whether they want to, or can, stay in business. However, you can't do that. Your household is your business, and you need to make it work.

Your budget is your plan for spending. Its purpose is to plan income and expenses, then track them with the idea of trying to maximize discretionary cash. It is a living, breathing document that needs to be monitored and adjusted as needed.

Monitoring Your Expenses

Your budget shows how you plan your expenses. You'll need to keep the books to determine if the money is indeed being spent for your budgeted items. There are many ways of doing this.

1. Develop a simple Excel spreadsheet to keep track of expenditures. Figure 3-3 shows an example of this.

2. Alternatively, you can keep track of your budget without a computer. The simplest way is to get a Cash Book/Journal from an office supply store. This is usually a 7X12- inch hardcover book with two columns on the left side and two columns on the right side. Have a separate page for each expense. At the top of each page, list the expense to be followed on that page, and head the far right column with the amount budgeted annually for that expense. In the other columns, list the date of payment,

Figure 3-3
Example of Monitoring a Budgeted Expense

BUDGET ITEM: RENT			
Budgeted Amount			$10,320
Date	Check Number	Amount	Balance
1/1/2008	478	$860	$9,460
2/4/2008	485	$860	$8,600
3/2/2008	498	$860	$7,740

the check number, and any other information you deem necessary. In the second-from-right column, show the amount paid for that month, and subtract that from the balance of the account in the far-right column. Thus, you can see the monthly drawdown for this expense account.

3. If you want to spend a little money on it, there are numerous software packages, such as Quicken, which have all kinds of budgeting aids for you. Also, many banks and credit unions offer free personal finance software to their customers.

It is important that you monitor your expenses each month to ensure that you are spending your money as budgeted.

Lisa and Morgan's Cash Flow Statement
Let's take a look at Figure 3-4, the Cash Flow Statement of the couple from Chapter 2, Lisa and Morgan Silverod. You'll remember that this couple had a negative net worth of $1,553.

A Problem in Handling Money
Wow! Last year they spent $24,572 more than they earned. No wonder they had a negative net worth. This is really a shame. They are both pulling in decent salaries, $175,750 for the two of them, but apparently they've been spending too much for a long time. They've been living high on the hog, but the hog has gone wild. And because they are so deeply indebted to others,

Figure 3-4

Lisa and Morgan Silverod
Cash Flow Statement, 2008

CASH IN	
Salary (Lisa)	$90,000
Salary (Morgan)	85,750
Interest	97

CASH OUT	TOTAL CASH IN	$175,847
401(k), Lisa	$1,000	
401(k), Morgan	1,200	
Automobile (Fuel, Insurance, Maintenance, Tag, and Tax)	8,694	
Boat Payments	3,500	
Cable TV/Internet	1,900	
Car Payments	12,042	
Chartitable Contributions	5,000	
Clothing	9,500	
Credit Card Payments	12,042	
Electricity	1,963	
Entertainment/Dining Out	12,000	
Federal Income Taxes	31,606	
Food	7,500	
Gifts	4,600	
Health Insurance	3,450	
House Insurance	4,480	
House Maintenance	4,800	
Medical/Dental	1,800	
Mortgage (Principal and Interest)	26,935	
Property Taxes	6,500	
Pocket Money	8,000	
RV Payments	2,440	
Second Mortgage Payments (P and I)	1,954	
Social Security/Medicare	12,393	
State Income Taxes	2,780	
Telephone	1,680	
Veterinary Payments	300	
Vacations	10,000	
Water/Sewage	360	
TOTAL CASH OUT	$200,419	
CASH FLOW	($24,572)	

it's not even their hog they're riding. They need to rein in their spending, or prepare to live life on the brink of economic failure. However, they are young, and can improve their situation in time.

They need a budget very badly. I suspect that they have not ever had one, nor have really ever paid any attention to how much they were spending. This is a recipe for a financial disaster.

Spend Less and Reduce Debt

In preparing for their financial success, they need to improve their spending habits. The first thing is to get rid of a lot of that debt they are carrying. Referring to their Net Worth Statement from Chapter Two, you'll see that, excluding the mortgage loan, they have a total debt of $143,047 when they combine their RV, boat, and car loans with their credit card debt. That must be paid down as quickly as possible. It will take a few years, but it needs to start immediately. They will need to sell some things, as well as cut back on non-essential items to pay off this debt. By the time they have made a dent in their credit card debt, their car loans should be paid off, and that will be a relief, of course. Now, let's see how they might proceed in reducing their debt.

Sell Some Assets

The first thing they need to do is sell the RV and the boat. At this time in their lives, they just can't afford them. These possessions are making them poor. Sale of the RV and the boat will bring in $33,500 in additional cash. This can be used to pay off the loan balances of $28,750, and leave $4,750 to help pay off some of the credit card debt.

Cut Expenses

On the Cash Flow Statement, there are several obvious expense items that could be cut immediately. Table 3-5 shows four of them.

These four items total $39,500, and they seem to have a discretionary aspect to them. Entertaining and dining out can be done at home, costing a fraction of the $12,000 they spent last year. Similarly, clothing could be cut back somewhat. Apparently, they took a grand and expensive vacation last year, spending $10,000. Perhaps next year, their vacation could be more modest. And finally, there's the pocket money of $8,000. This is about $77 per week for each of them. That seems like a lot of money. I wonder if they know what they are spending it on.

These four items can be cut by $21,000, as shown in Table 3-5. This amount can be applied to reducing their debt, starting with the credit card debt on which interest is being charged at a rate of 15%. The removal of this debt will not be accomplished in one year, but it's a start. And as 6th Century B.C. Chinese philosopher Lao-tzu would remind us, a journey of a thousand miles begins with a single step.

Table 3-5
Cutback in Spending for Lisa and Morgan

EXPENSE ITEM	2007 SPENT	AMOUNT CUT	2008 BUDGET
Entertainment/Dining out	$12,000	$8,000	$4,000
Clothing	9,500	2,000	7,500
Vacations	10,000	8,000	2,000
Pocket Money	8,000	3,000	5,000
Totals	$39,500	$21,000	$18,500

Lisa and Morgan's Budget

Figure 3-6 shows the extension of their 2008 cash flow statement to their 2009 budget. They are planning to sell their RV and boat. They are expecting salary increases for the next year, and that is included in their 2008 budget. Estimated adjustments are made for the increase in federal and state income taxes withheld, and the payroll taxes. Then the cutbacks for

Figure 3-6
Lisa and Morgan Silverod

CASH IN	2008 CASH FLOW	CHANGES	2009 BUDGET
Salary (Lisa)	$90,000	$2,000	$92,000
Salary (Morgan)	85,750	1,250	87,000
Sale of RV		13,000	13,000
Sale of Boat		20,500	20,500
Interest	97	10	107
TOTAL CASH IN	$175,847		$212,607
CASH OUT			
401(k), Lisa	$1,000		$1,000
401(k), Morgan	1,200		1,200
Automobile (Fuel, Insurance, Maintenance, Tax, Tag)	8,694		8,694
Boat Loan Payoff		15,000	15,000
Boat Payments	3,500		0
Cable TV/Internet	1,900		1,900
Car Payments	12,042		12,042
Chartitable Contributions	5,000		5,000
Clothing	9,500	-2,000	7,500
Credit Card Payments	12,042	8,369	20,411
Electricity	1,900		1,900
Entertainment/Dining Out	12,000	-8,000	4,000
Federal Income Taxes	31,606	553	32,159
Food	7,500		7,500
Gifts	4,600		4,600
Health Insurance	3,450		3,450
House Insurance	4,480		4,480
House Maintenance	4,800		4,800
Medical/Dental	1,800		1,800
Mortgage Payments (Principal and Interest)	26,935		26,935
Property Taxes	6,500		6,500
Pocket Money	8,000	-3,000	5,000
RV Loan Payoff		13,750	13,750
RV Payments	2,440		0
Second Mortgage Payments (P and I)	1,954		1,954
Social Security/Medicare	12,393	289	12,682
State Income Taxes	2,780	293	3,073
Telephone	1,680		1,680
Vacations	10,000	-8,000	2,000
Veterinary Payments	300		300
Water/Sewage	360		360
TOTAL CASH OUT	$200,419		$212,607
NET CASH FLOW	($24,572)		0

items listed in Table 3-5 were implemented, which reduced their expenses by $21,000.

By selling and paying off the two non-essential items, the RV and the boat, and by the implementation of the cutbacks, they have started reducing their debt. But most importantly, they have stemmed the tide of deficit spending. These are important first steps. Now, what they are going to need to do is stop spending so much money and whittle down their debt so they can start saving and investing. Without a plan for saving and investing, they will never be financially successful.

The next two chapters will present ideas on how to avoid wasting money and how to spend in order to get the most value from the expenditure. Following these recommendations will result in less cash outflow, and increase the discretionary cash available to accumulate wealth.

CHAPTER FOUR
GETTING MORE BANG FOR THE BUCK

In the preceding two chapters, we developed your Net Worth Statement, Cash Flow Statement, and Budget. Also, we introduced the idea that reducing your expenses is an important way of achieving positive cash flow, or increasing your already positive cash flow. This chapter will give you ideas on how to increase the value you get from your expenditures. In other words, how to get your money's worth. I call this "getting more bang for the buck." Stated more formally, you need to be value conscious.

Chapter Five will give you ideas on how to avoid wasting money. If you incorporate the ideas from these two chapters into your spending patterns, you will increase your positive cash flow.

Price and Value

Price and value are sometimes confused with one another. Price refers to the cost, or the dollar amount, of a purchase. In general, the lower the price, the more appealing a purchase might be. Value refers to whether you are paying an appropriate price for an item of a given quality. Paying $10 for a shoddy item considers price alone. Paying $15 for a quality item may be better in the long run. When you consider price alone, you are not shopping well. There's an old adage, "You get what you pay for." In general, this is true. But a really good deal happens when you buy a quality item for a bargain price. And of course, the purchase should be for something that you need or want. That leads us to the next section.

> ## A Really Good Deal
>
> When you buy a quality item for a bargain price, you've found a value buy.

What to Buy

Before buying something, the first consideration is to ascertain its value to you. Purchases should be made according to a hierarchy:

1. Needs
2. Reasonable wants
3. Less-than-reasonable wants
4. Whims

First, buy what you need. Then, finances permitting, buy what is a reasonable want. Then, again, finances permitting, buy a less-that-reasonable item that is still something you want. As for purchasing whims, wait until you are financially secure and stable before doing this.

Problems occur when purchases are made that violate this hierarchy. The following ideas are for spending money on needs and reasonable wants.

Your Car

The purchase and ownership of a vehicle is a major item in a household's budget. Here are some ideas for doing it right.

Buy the right car

- Don't buy more car than you need.
- If you are a household of two, a sedan or coupe will probably work nicely for you.
- If you are a household of three or four, an SUV might be best.
- If you need to haul things for your vocation or your avocation, probably a pick-up truck will fit the bill.
- And buy a quality car, one that will be reliable and not drain your resources. Check *Consumer Reports*[1] to see the repair record of the year, make, and model you are

---

1 *Consumer Reports* is a periodical published by Consumers Union. It accepts no advertising and gives objective and unbiased information of value to a consumer. Most libraries have it in their reference section.

considering. Complete car reports are available online at **www.consumerreports.org**.

Buy It Right

- It makes most sense to buy a late-model used car. About 20% of a new car's value evaporates when it is driven off the dealer's lot. By purchasing a car that is one or two years old, you let the original buyer take the depreciation hit, and you get a better deal.
- But caution: know from whom you are buying. Some people buy a new car with the idea of having it for a year or two, and abuse it by not maintaining it properly or, if living in a cold climate, racing a cold engine. You don't want to buy that car.
- Buying from a new car dealer (unlike buying from a private party) will give you some recourse if things go wrong.
- Also, with a new car dealer, buying a late-model car just off a lease can be a good purchase.
- Many people have success buying a car from nationally-known used car companies. These firms check their cars very carefully, performing many tests to ensure they are selling vehicles that run well, and they often have policies of making good on repairs that are needed immediately. Two useful websites are **www.carmax.com** and **www.autonation.com**.
- Understand that when buying a car from a dealer, you, an amateur buyer, are talking to a professional seller. You need to do some homework before you meet the salesperson. See **www.cars.com** for useful background information.
- Go into a transaction with knowledge of the car's Blue Book value. Two websites, **www.edmunds.com** or **www.KBB.com**, show prices expected from private parties and dealers on virtually all cars. With this information, you will be in a better bargaining position.

- When negotiating a trade-in deal, keep the cost of the car you want to buy separate from a discussion of the trade-in value a dealer will give you on your present car. Mixing the two can easily cause confusion.

Don't Lease a New Car

It may be tempting to lease a new car rather than buying one, especially if the monthly lease payments are less than what the payments on a car loan might be. I don't recommend leasing a car for these reasons:

- In your lease payments, you are paying for the car's depreciation, and that is substantial.
- If you buy a brand new car, you'll take the hit on depreciation, but if you keep the car for some time, that depreciation can be spread over your ownership period to make it less burdensome.
- You are responsible for the terms of the lease that may include maintenance, mileage, and other restrictions. If you don't follow the terms of the lease, you may have a surcharge when the leasing period is over.
- When the lease period is over, you turn the car in. Now you don't have a car, and will have to lease or buy another one. Leasing is usually a better deal for the lessor than you.
- Lease payments are like rent. You have no ownership. And although monthly lease payments may be lower than the payments on a regular auto loan, when the leasing period is over, you have nothing. With car payments, at least you have some equity in the car, and when the loan is paid off, you own the car.

> **Take Note**
>
> Leasing a new car is usually more expensive in the long run.

Insurance

In many states, you cannot register your car unless you can show proof of insurance. Aside from this legal requirement, you need insurance coverage to protect you from liability if you have an accident. So, buy it, have it, but seek value in it.

- Shop around for the best price on the coverage that you want. Go to **www.naic.org** to find out your state's insurance commission website, and get some guidance from that on policy costs and coverage.
- Is your car an older one, perhaps without very much cash value? See if your policy includes comprehensive and collision coverage. If so, ask yourself if you really need it. Probably not.
- If you have small claims from time to time, it might be better to absorb them, rather than take them to the insurance company. Your rates may increase from numerous small claims. Save the insurance claims for the big stuff.
- If you're a careful driver who doesn't get into many accidents, consider raising the deductible to at least $500. Your premium will be reduced considerably.
- Also, insurers often give discounts for covering cars with anti-lock brakes, covering two cars in the same household, or covering a car in conjunction with a homeowner's or renter's policy. See if discounts are available. Rate quotes are available online at **www.carinsurancerates.com**.

General Purchasing

How you go about shopping will determine in part how well you'll be spending your money.

Where and When to Shop

- Do some investigating as to the best places to shop for various items. The best places have a combination of good quality, low prices, and decent service.
- Warehouse clubs like Sam's and Costco often meet these criteria. Just be careful not to buy more than you need just because the items are sold in bulk.

When You Buy

Do the math. What is your purchase really going to cost?

- Do research online to find out which places have the best prices on items you want to buy. Even if you don't buy them online, when you go into a store to make your actual purchase, you will have some idea of what to look for, and you'll know what range of prices to expect.
- Try to buy off-season. Rakes, trowels, and other gardening equipment will have lower prices in the fall than in the spring. Likewise, toys and games will be better priced in January than in December. And remember that matinee ticket prices at the movies are usually cheaper than evening prices.

How to Pay for Your Purchases

When you purchase an item, you have several choices on how to pay for it. The next chapter is devoted to the good and bad usages of credit cards, so I'll not get into that now. Beyond credit cards, however, there are three possibilities that present themselves.

Pay Cash

Paying cash is fine. More people should do it.

Before the widespread use of credit cards, this is the way most people bought and paid for things. You went to a store, selected an item to purchase, and paid for it with greenbacks or a personal check. And, in most cases, if you were pleased with your purchase and had no need for an exchange or refund, the transaction was completed. In fact, as we will see in Chapter Six, if you have made many purchases and have abused your credit card by running up a sizable debt, this may be the best way to discipline yourself.

Layaway Purchases

A layaway purchase is a plan used by customers who want to buy an item, but don't have the entire amount of money needed for the purchase. A customer selects an item, makes a payment of a percentage of the cost, and the retailer "lays away" the item. Then, over a period of weeks or months, payments are made by the customer until the entire amount of the purchase is paid. Then, the customer receives the item purchased. And, as is the case with a cash purchase described above, if the customer was pleased with the purchase, and had no need for an exchange or refund, the transaction was completed. This was sometimes described as buying something "on time."

Layaways Are a Discipline

The number of stores offering layaway plans has decreased over the past decade, largely due to an increased use of credit cards. Yet, layaway is a viable option if you don't have the cash and you don't need the item right away. In essence, you are saving to buy the items for cash, but you are having the store keep the money while you are saving. Frequently, there are no charges assessed by the retailer. However, you don't earn any interest on the money left with the establishment.

Another benefit of this plan is that, if used to purchase an item in short supply, it can guarantee that the item will be available to you when you pay it off. At holiday time, this might be a consideration with popular electronics or toys.

Make Sure You Understand the Terms

You can avoid problems by understanding the agreement you have with the retailer, and understanding the risks involved. Here are some considerations:
- Are there costs involved?
- When are the payments due?
- Are there charges for late payments?
- What happens if you don't complete your payments?
- What is the retailer's refund policy?

And, of course, be sure you are dealing with an established and reputable merchant. The last thing you want is to be almost through with the payments, and then find out the merchant has gone bankrupt.

Rent-to-Own
This is usually a very bad idea.

Some people want to purchase an item immediately, but don't have the cash and don't have a credit card on which to charge the purchase. But they do have a steady job that gives them steady income. They can buy the item at a rent-to-own business. They receive the item right away and make weekly payments to the retailer, as per the agreement. The problem is that the total amount they end up paying can greatly exceed the price of the item.

For example, they can rent a $350 electronic game, and make $25 weekly payments over the standard period of 30 weeks. They will have paid $750 ($25 times 30 weeks) for the purchase of an item costing $350. Thus, a $350 purchase morphs into a $750 one. The actual cost paid represents 214% of the item's original cost. Not a good deal.

I don't recommend doing this. If you want to purchase something, pay cash - either greenbacks or check - or put it on your credit card with the idea of paying off the entire card balance at the end of the month. It's a lot cheaper that way.

Total Cost and Making Payments
People who make purchases at a rent-to-own business are falling into an easy trap. They are looking at payments rather than total cost. And is it any wonder they might think that way? You pick up a newspaper and it states that you can buy, say, a car for monthly payments of $439 or lease the car for $375 per month. Frequently, there is no mention of the total cost or the interest to be paid, or the period of the loan. And if there is, it's usually buried in the fine print.

A person can look at the size of the monthly payment, consider the size of his or her monthly salary and existing financial obligations, and say, "Hmm. $439 a month? I can handle that." And so they can, but at what total cost? You could probably afford to pay $439 a month for the rest of your life, but is that what you want to do?

You're Probably Overpaying

Some companies can snooker you by focusing on the monthly payments, and not the car's total price. You need to be concerned with the total amount of money the item will have cost you when the last payment is made.

The rent-to-own syndrome – considering the purchase in terms of your cash going out on a monthly basis rather than the total cost of the purchase – will result in overpaying. You are not getting value for your money. You are getting <u>less</u> bang for the buck, and I recommend that you <u>not</u> do this.

Charitable Giving

One of the nice things about having some discretionary cash is that you can give some of it away. There are many worthy causes to which you can give. Our government provides an incentive for us to give to charity, by allowing us a deduction on our federal income taxes for donations to qualified organizations. Such organizations are referred to as 501(c)(3) entities, named after the section of tax code that authorizes them. But the real reason for giving is that it's the right thing to do. I recommend that you do it, but do it carefully, so you know that your money is being deployed as you intended.

Is it a Charity?

People may come to your door seeking a cash contribution of some amount. Some are legitimate and some are not. Two real-life anecdotes exemplify this.

Sometime around 1974, while living in Indiana, a girl around age 16 came to my doorstep, asking for money so she and some friends could take a trip to Acapulco. I politely declined. Then, a few minutes later, I thought to myself, "What nerve! She wanted me, a perfect stranger, to finance a fun trip for herself and some friends." At least she was honest about it. Obviously, her planned trip was not a legitimate charity.

Cash Donations
Also not a legitimate charity was the man who came to my door-step a few years later, in the midst of a deep recession, seeking a contribution for "homeless victims." He had in his hand an envelope with some cash visible. I excused myself for a moment, and then gave him a check for $10. The check never cleared the bank. All I can say positive about him is that he was smart. By never cashing the check, he left no paper trail for someone to use to expose his fraud.

Beyond these bizarre and somewhat obvious bad examples, there are many legitimate charities to which you might make a contribution. But will your money go toward the stated purpose of the charity? This is a concern, because there are charities in which almost half of all donations go to administrative and fund-raising costs.

Investigate Before You Donate
The Better Business Bureau Standards for Charitable Account-ability state that 65% or more of the money given to the char-ity should go to fund its programs, and that no more than 35% should go toward administrative and fundraising expense. I feel this is somewhat low. I'd prefer to have 85% of donations go toward its programs. In any case, the American Institute of Philanthropy recommends that you "investigate before you donate." Sage advice. Check it out at **www.charitywatch.org**.

In general, I prefer to make contributions by check for two rea-sons. First, you'll have a record of the contribution. And second, cash donations sometimes mysteriously disappear. The love of money can be a strong incentive for mischief.

Minimizing Your Taxes

Expenses for taxes represent a significant portion of the overall expense of a household. While it is your duty as a citizen to pay the taxes you owe, it does you no good to overpay by not taking advantage of the ways you can minimize your tax burden. Here are some suggestions.

- There are many nationally branded tax services that will fill out your tax returns for a fee. If you are tax-phobic, you might avail yourself of their services. But note that at tax time, in March or April of each year, they increase their staff to service all their customers. Not all persons on their staff are fully qualified to handle complicated tax returns.
- There are several software packages, such as TurboTax or TaxCut, which allow you to complete your own tax forms independently.
- Your employment may offer several ways to reduce your taxes. There are tax-free flexible spending accounts, in which you can take benefits rather than cash, tax-free accident and medical insurance, and educational programs.
- Also, contributions to tax-favored retirement plans, such as a 401(k) and employee stock purchase plans, will reduce your taxes.
- When filing your taxes, you have a choice between taking the standard deduction and itemizing deductions. If you want to itemize deductions, it might help to "bunch" them in one year, rather than spread them out in several years. You can do this with charitable giving or by prepaying property taxes, for instance. By bunching them, you might have enough deductions to exceed the threshold (which will vary among tax returns) that would allow the benefits of itemizing. Then, in the years in which you have fewer deductions, use the standard deduction.

Dining Out and Eating Out

First let's make a distinction between <u>eating</u> out and <u>dining</u> out. Eating out is what you do when someone else prepares the food. Dining out is a kind of eating out, but it is in a nice restaurant, and is an unhurried and perhaps social experience.

Eating Out

You come home from work. You're tired. You have not planned anything for dinner. So you say, "Let's eat out." In other words, "I'm too tired to cook anything. Let someone else cook." There is no ceremony, no festivity, no social occasion. You just need to eat something because you're hungry. You have several choices. You can eat at a fast food restaurant. You can get take-out at a supermarket. For example, pick up a rotisserie chicken and a couple of sides. Or you can order-in a pizza or something like that. Take-out or order-in is convenient and usually fairly inexpensive, and for a takeout order, there is no tip involved.

Dining Out

Dining out is different from eating out. Often you want to do this with friends and enjoy yourself. You can and should do this, but you can really reduce the cost of the experience by following a few simple suggestions.

Here's one idea. Let's say you are going to dine out with another couple. Try this:

1. Meet at your place. Provide drinks and snacks. Appoint a designated driver. Everyone can drink alcohol except the DD.
2. Go to the restaurant as a foursome. Order entrees, but no drinks or appetizers. (You did that at your place.)
3. Return to your place (or their place) for coffee and dessert.

> **Budget Tip**
>
> **Let the restaurant prepare entrees. You can do everything else.**

Following these suggestions can save you a lot of money, and you can still have a nice time. I call this "modified dining out."

Table 4-1
Comparison of Costs of
Dining Out and Modified Dining Out

FOOD OR DRINK ITEM	RESTAURANT COST	HOME COST
6 drinks @ $7 each	$42	$10
4 Appetizers @ $5 each	20	10
4 Entrees @ $20 each	80	80
4 Desserts @ $6 each	24	8
4 Coffees @ $4 each	16	1
Subtotal	182	109
Gratuity @ 17%	31	14
Total Cost for Four People	213	123
Your Cost for You as a Couple	107	62

An Example of Modified Dining Out

Let's say you are going to dine out with friends, another couple. You decide to follow these three suggestions above, and have drinks, appetizers, coffee, and desserts at home, while having the entrées at the restaurant. Table 4-1, using round and approximate numbers, shows the difference in cost.

So, your share of the evening's festivities is $62 rather than $107. It really makes a lot of sense to dine out this way. The restaurant makes most of its money not on their entrées, but rather on the items that accompany them. But you probably are not dining out for those items. It's probably the entrées that you really want. This is getting more bang for the buck.

Did You Know This?

It might be of interest and useful to know the difference between the cost of drinks at a restaurant and the retail cost of drinks for in-home consumption. *The Wall Street Journal*[2] reports that the standard price for a bottle of wine at a restaurant is about twice the retail price you'd pay at a store. And wine

2   August 15, 2008

by the glass is "priced aggressively." Indeed, often it's cheaper to buy a more expensive wine by the bottle than to buy a cheaper wine by the glass. As for beer and liquor, the restaurant markups can be 500% or more.

Large Portions at the Restaurant
Here's another idea. Let's say the two of you want to dine out. If you dine at a restaurant that serves generous portions, you might want to order one appetizer and one entrée, and split them. In addition to saving money, this might cut down on your consumption of food, and help you control your weight.

Eating In
Eating in probably has the least cash outlay of any eating options. If you have the time, or can make the time, it can be well worth it. But try to use your time wisely. At home, try this. If you are going to make lasagna for the two of you, make a quadruple recipe that will serve perhaps 16. Eat some that night, put another night's portion in the fresh food section of your refrigerator, then portion up the rest, wrap them in aluminum foil with labels as to the contents and date, and freeze them for future consumption. It takes just a touch more time to make 16 servings than it does to make two servings. Then, some time next week, when you leave for work in the morning, take out a frozen portion and put it in the fresh food section of the fridge. When you come home from work, nuke it and serve it.

At Work
In your normal day, you probably take a break for lunch. If you can bring your lunch, ("brown-bagging" it), you can save a considerable amount of money, perhaps $7-$10 or more per day. Do the math. Five days per week times 50 weeks times $7 is $1,750. The cost of the food for your lunch is probably negligible compared to eating out.

If you eat lunch alone, you might as well brown-bag it. But is lunch a social event for you? A time to share with your co-workers? Perhaps they would like to do the same. Perhaps you all could take turns bringing lunch, hot or cold. In addition to saving money, you can more easily control the portions to keep your weight down.

At the Supermarket

When grocery shopping, you can save a lot of money by following just a few common sense suggestions.

- Plan menus for the week. This will allow you to do one major shopping trip per week and buy what you need.
- Keep a running shopping list, especially for staples like crackers or mustard, for example.
- When you shop, keep to your list. That will reduce your purchases of potato chips and other junk food.
- Don't shop when you're hungry or tired. You'll probably buy more than you need.
- If you have coupons from the newspaper, direct mail, or online, use them. Clip them onto your shopping list. But be careful. Use them for items you would have purchased anyway.
- Follow the advertised specials, but again, only buy items that you would have purchased anyway.
- The lowest priced items are usually found on the lower shelves.
- House brands, especially for things like dishwasher detergent, are usually as good as national brands.
- Be careful about purchasing non-food items in supermarkets. Food items typically have low mark-ups, while non-food items have higher mark-ups, and supermarkets are increasingly making these high mark-up products available to shoppers. A furnace filter in a supermarket can cost twice as much as from a hardware store.
- Also, don't buy better than you need. For example, if you only use paper towels to clean your car windows, you probably don't need the strength of a national brand.

Cash Management

How you manage your cash will have a great impact on your financial well-being. Here are some suggestions.

- Have a checking account that pays you interest. As I write these words, most checking accounts pay 0.25% or 0.50%. This is not a lot of money, but it's something, and better than nothing.
- If you can pay your bills by a direct bank draft, do it. You will save on the cost of the checks you might have written, and the postage to send them.
- If you have a choice as to when to pay the bills, select the latest possible date to pay without penalty. In this way, your checking account will have the money longer, and you will receive more interest than you might have received by paying earlier.
- Do you use an ATM for your immediate cash needs? Do they charge you a fee for such usage? Many banks do. I know people who need $20 for a week's pocket money, and will get it from an ATM that charges them $3.00 per transaction. That's a 15% charge. Do that once a week and you will have paid $156 for the year.
- Here's a better idea: Anticipate your cash needs for the month. Let's say it's about $20 per week. Then make one withdrawal from the ATM of $100. Put $20 in your pocket, and put the rest in an envelope in your sock drawer. Take out cash when you need it. You'll lose a few pennies of interest that the cash in the envelope might have earned, but you will have avoided $12 in transaction costs.
- Or even better yet, go to your bank and write a check for $100 in cash and avoid the ATM transaction fee altogether. Or get cash back from a bank deposit or at the supermarket.

The next chapter continues our quest for increasing cash flow by decreasing wasteful spending.

CHAPTER FIVE
WASTE NOT, WANT NOT

In the summer of 2008, T. Boone Pickens, octogenarian billionaire oilman from Texas, was testifying before a U.S. Senate committee, giving his views on an energy policy for the United States. He was asked about the importance of conservation, and he answered that it was "number one" of all the issues involved. He told about his childhood when he would visit his grandmother. One time he left a room without turning off the lights. His grandmother said, "If you do that again, I'm going to give you the electric bill." Senator Lieberman, a member of the committee, volunteered shortly thereafter, "I had a grandmother like that, too."

Well, so did I.

The Senior Generation

Pickens, Lieberman, and I share one thing in common. We three are from a generation that didn't have much to begin with, and were taught not to waste things. We were taught this not as a one-time event, but rather as a way of life.

In the Great Depression of the 1930s, food and consumer goods cost money that many people didn't have. Some children were taught the adage, "Waste not, want not." Other children were taught the verse, "Use it up/Wear it out/Make it do/Or do without." These children developed habits that would serve them well when they wanted to build wealth. They are your parents, grandparents, and great-grandparents. Although in this 21st century there is much more wealth to be had, and by many more people, we can learn some important lessons from them in terms of using our available resources.

Now, I'm not advocating a Spartan life style. I'm just empha-sizing using what you have effectively, and not wasting. As an example of what I mean, consider the plight of Germany after World War II. The economy was in shambles. There was hardly enough food to feed the civilian population. In 1945, above Army cafeteria-style mess hall lines in occupied Germany, there appeared signs stating, "Take all you want, but eat all you take." Wasting food in those circumstances would be deplorable. Some people believe that it is a sin to waste food, given the nutritional condition of most people in the world.

Isn't This Petty?

Many of the ideas presented in this chapter might seem petty. And, no doubt, some of them are. But in personal finance, if you take care of the nickels and dimes, the dollars will take care of themselves. Everett Dirksen, the late senator from Illinois, was referring to this idea (but, of course, on a different scale), when he humorously admonished his free-spending colleagues by stating, "A billion here, a billion there, pretty soon you're talking about real money."

Wasting is not just the wrong thing to do from a financial point of view, but from a moral point of view as well, as will be devel-oped later. So let's see how we can save some money by using resources wisely, not in a wasteful manner.

In Your Car

As I write, fuel costs are settling in the range of $3.50 to $4 per gallon. The era of cheap gas seems to be over. There are many things you can do to save money on fuel for your car.

Is This Trip Necessary?
- If you can walk a few blocks to pick up a three-ounce pre-scription at the drugstore, does it really make sense to move a 3,000-pound vehicle to accomplish that task? If you could walk it, then you should. Not only will you save gas, but you'll get some exercise as well.

Yes, This Trip Is Necessary

- Okay, if the trip is necessary (too far to walk, to heavy a load to carry, etc.) could you take public transportation? If not, and you need to take your car, can you combine this trip with other trips that are also necessary? Think about the varied trips you make in a given week. There may be some patterns there.
- Plan your trips so that you cover the fewest miles traveled and do all the trips at one time. There's a reason for this. A car engine is very inefficient until it is warmed up. It uses a lot of fuel when cold. If you have ten miles of driving to do in order to run three errands and you make three separate trips, you may have three separate cold starts, thus using a lot more fuel than doing the three errands consecutively with only one cold start.
- Also, by combining the errands, you'll save time.
- Try to avoid rush hours, or other times of peak road usage. Stop-and-go driving uses a lot of gas. Also, it's not much fun.

Buy the right grade of gasoline

- Are you buying premium or mid-range (94 or 89 octane) fuel for your car? Could it run just as well on regular (87 octane)? Check your owner's manual and see what it recommends. If it recommends 87 octane, use that.
- The savings can be significant when purchasing regular grade gasoline. If you drive 15,000 miles annually, and your car gets 25 miles per gallon, you use 600 gallons of gas per year. Do the math: 600 gallons times $3.75 per gallon costs $2,250 per year. The same amount of gas at $3.85 per gallon costs $2,310. You've wasted $60.
- You don't get any additional power by using a higher octane. If the manual recommends an octane higher than 87, try mixing what you're using with a half tank of a lower octane and see how it runs. You can always go back to an all-premium tank if you don't like the performance.

Drive Smart

- When accelerating from a complete stop, apply your foot gradually on the gas pedal, and increase the pressure as the transmission changes gears. This procedure uses much less gas than a jackrabbit start, and you will have a much smoother ride. Save your "lead foot" for passing on a two-lane road, or for merging into highway traffic.
- It takes a lot of gas to get a car moving. When it's already moving, it takes much less gas to keep it moving. So, try to pace yourself in terms of traffic in front of you. Also, anticipate the oncoming traffic lights, and try to get to them when they are green.
- Keep a safe distance between your car and the one in front of you – that is, don't tailgate. If the person in the car in front of you brakes hard, you can still stop in time without having to brake the same way
- It makes no sense to accelerate into a red light. Traffic permitting, when you see the light turn red as you're coming close to it, slow down by coasting with your foot ready to brake when needed.
- Think about it: every time you brake your car, you're wasting power already invested in the car's motion. So, the less you have to brake, the more efficiently you'll be using the power already spent.
- Keep your speed down. Wind resistance (drag) increases exponentially as your car goes faster. The difference in gas consumption between driving at 65 m.p.h. and 75 m.p.h. is significant.

Other car savings

- If you like your car, keep it well maintained. A little prevention can cut down on a lot of repairs. Regular maintenance can prolong you car's life. The website **www.cartalk.com** has a listing of "above average" mechanics in your area.

> ### Pay Attention!
> **Your car has the potential to be a money hog.**

- When something goes wrong with your car, fix it. If you don't, its repair needs will pile up, and suddenly you'll realize that you're driving a piece of junk and may need to buy a new car. Besides, there are safety issues to consider.
- If you use your car trunk for storage, don't. It takes additional power to haul things around. Keep only essential items in your trunk.
- Don't bother with gas or oil additives unless recommended by a trustworthy mechanic. Typically, they have no effect on the performance of your car.
- Be sure that your tires are inflated properly. Too low pressure can increase rolling resistance and lower your MPG.
- If the outside air temperature is pleasant, drive around with the windows open when in town, or just have the fan on. But on the highway, keep the windows closed. Open windows will reduce your gas mileage by increasing drag.
- Don't "warm up" your car by letting it idle after you start it (unless you live in a sub-zero climate and your car doesn't have a warming device). Modern car engines and multi-grade oils make this unnecessary, and you'll only be wasting gas. But keep your engine speed (RPMs) low for the first minute or so.
- If you come to a railroad crossing and a long train is on the tracks, and you know you'll be waiting for some time, turn the engine off. The same goes for other instances, such as waiting outside a school to pick up a child. You'll save fuel and reduce pollution as well.

At Home

Doing some simple things in your home can save a great amount of money.

- Make sure your house is sealed up properly and that there are no cracks through which outside air (hot or cold) can enter. Use weather-stripping around outside doors and windows, and caulk up the cracks.

- You can check for leaks by lighting a candle, and bringing it near doors and windows. If the flame flickers, you probably have a leak that needs fixing.
- If you own your own home, it will pay off in the long run to have the walls and roof insulated. If it snowed last night and there is no snow on your roof, you probably lack roof insulation.
- Turn off the lights and the TV or radio when you leave a room for anything more than a few minutes.
- Replace standard incandescent bulbs with compact fluorescent light bulbs. They cost a bit more, but the savings in electricity are significant, and because they last longer, you don't have to replace them as often.
- Your refrigerator uses an enormous amount of energy. Try to put things in the same place in the fridge, so you don't have to go searching for items while the door is open.
- Turn the thermostat down when you leave the house for the day, and during sleeping hours.
- While in the house, keep your thermostat set so you are comfortable, but the rooms are not overly warm or cold.
- Change your furnace or air conditioner filters frequently, at least two or three times a year, and even more when the heating and cooling appliances are under continuous usage.
- In the summer, if you have light-colored blinds, close them during the time the sun shines on the window. The light will be reflected back outside, and it will take the strain off the air conditioner.
- And during the winter, allow the sun to pour into your rooms. This will help heat the house.
- When guests are leaving your abode, say your goodbyes before they step out the door, or right after, but with the door shut. That way, less heated or cooled air will be lost.
- When you buy a new or replacement appliance (washer, dryer, dishwasher, etc.), buy one with resource-saving features. New appliances use less electricity, water and

gas, and the savings over time can be substantial.

- Also, if buying a freezer, buy a chest freezer, rather than an upright model. Cooler air flows downward, and an upright model loses a lot of cool air when the door is opened. Much less, if any, cool air is lost when opening a chest freezer.
- Generally, don't buy extended warranties. The warranty that comes with the purchase of an appliance is usually in effect for one year. If there are problems with an appliance, they will usually show up during the first year, and you are covered. And if problems don't show up in a year, they probably will not show up in the useful life of the appliance. Extended warranties are usually not worth their cost.

Other ideas for achieving energy efficiency in your home can be found at **www.energysavers.gov**.

Keep Healthy

In Chapter Nine, I present material about health insurance. I recommend that you have it, either through your employment, or purchased privately. Without it, you face a potential financial catastrophe. But beyond this thought, being healthy and staying healthy is part of your financial success. Also, who wants to be sick if it can be avoided?

If you don't have any health insurance, a situation that I do <u>not</u> recommend, you'll have to pay for the medical services you receive directly out of your pocket. But even if you do indeed have such insurance, there are deductibles and co-payments that your insurance policy will not cover, and which will need to be paid by you.

There are some things you can do to stay healthy, to reduce these expenses as much as possible. As the old saying goes, "An ounce of prevention is worth a pound of cure." That's the key: prevention. Here are some ideas.

- Get annual check-ups. Many potentially serious conditions can be treated effectively if discovered early.
- Know your family history. Is there diabetes in your family? How about heart disease? Perhaps you have a predisposition toward a certain medical condition. By knowing your family history, you can be on the lookout for symptoms, which might reveal potential problems and allow them to be treated earlier.
- Keep fit. Most doctors agree that by keeping your weight down and getting some exercise on a daily basis, you can avoid many medical problems.
- Drink plenty of water. Water hydrates the skin, curbs the appetite, and helps remove toxins from your system. Most health professionals recommend eight 8-ounce glasses daily. That's two quarts. Coffee and colas do not count. Drink plain water, H2O. An extensive discussion about the health benefits of drinking water can be found at **www.heartspring.net**.
- Eat varied high fiber foods, including lots of fruits and vegetables, to aid your digestion.
- Drink coffee and alcohol in moderation, if at all. Excessive use of caffeine can cause heart problems, and of course, too much alcohol can severely and sometimes dangerously impair your behavior. Use of either can lead to dehydration. And if both are avoided within four hours of bedtime, you'll sleep better, too.
- Use sun block if you spend significant periods of time outdoors in daylight. Your face, especially your nose and ears, may be vulnerable to skin cancer from too much exposure to sun.
- Floss your teeth at least once daily. Many harmful bacteria colonize between the teeth, and on the teeth above or below the gum line. Flossing will reduce the presence of these bacteria, decrease the chances of gum diseases, and possibly help avoid heart disease.
- Do what you can to reduce stress in your life. Chronic stress is a killer. It can increase your chances of heart

disease, obesity, infections, and depression. Medical experts believe that 60-90% of illness is stress related.
- Try to get at least eight hours of uninterrupted sleep every day.

Water, Water, Everywhere

We are lucky in this country. In many places in the world, clean drinking water is hard to come by. But in our country, clean water is abundant and cheap. I mean tap water. Yet, many folks buy bottled water. Keeping well-hydrated is recommended by medical professionals, and water is the best hydration liquid. Tap water works as well as bottled water, and is a lot less expensive.

Twenty years ago, bottled water meant Evian or Perrier, mineral water bottled at the source. Often, people who were in a restaurant or bar and chose not to drink alcohol ordered this instead. It was considered very chic to order either of these two brands, a definite cut above ordering club soda or sparkling water.

Bottled Water: A New Profit Center

Then, about 1985, some marketing maven realized that selling bottled water would capitalize on the health concerns of young people, and a market developed for alternatives to colas and other soft drinks. And voila, bottled water came on the scene.

Bottled or Tap?

Does bottled water taste better than tap water? Most people can't tell the difference. I know I usually can't. Perhaps you saw the movie *Return to Me*, which has a memorable restaurant scene in which an obnoxious customer orders bottled water because she says she "can't stand" the taste of tap water. After having been treated shabbily by this woman, the waitress goes to the bar, takes a container of bottled water, empties it, and fills it with tap water. Then, she serves it to the same surly customer, who sips it and revels in how good it tastes.

Health and Cost

Is bottled water healthier than tap water? Probably not. In fact, drinking it may be detrimental to your dental health since it usually contains no fluoride, whereas most tap water does.

And then there's the cost. A six-pack of 16.9-ounce store-brand bottles of water costs $1.99 in my neighborhood. That's 1.96 cents per ounce. And, of course, a national brand of water costs even more. But let's focus on the store brand. Do the math. There are 128 ounces in a gallon, so 128 times $.0196 = $2.51. Thus, the cost of a gallon of bottled water is $2.51. In contrast, at water rates charged by a typical municipality, $2 will buy about 1,000 gallons of tap water. That computes to two-thousandths of one cent per ounce.

It wasn't long ago that a gallon of gasoline was selling for less than the $2.51 now charged for a gallon of bottled water. Now, as I write, gas is hovering at about $4 per gallon. That means the gallon of bottled water costs 63% of the cost of a gallon of gasoline.

My suggestion is that if your local water is good to drink, then drink lots of it, and don't buy bottled water. To do otherwise is just a waste of money. And besides, think of all those throwaway plastic bottles that are filling our landfills. They are made from petroleum, an increasingly scarce and expensive resource.

Wasting is a Moral Issue

In this chapter, we have explored ways of avoiding waste for the purpose of reducing our expenses and increasing our positive cash flow. And that is one of the purposes of this book. But there is another reason to avoid waste. It's the right thing to do.

Stewardship of the Earth's Resources

The world's resources are finite, and we are the current stewards for these resources. Our children and grandchildren will be taking over the stewardship when we shuffle off this mortal coil.

Are there enough resources for our successors and us? I don't know. Should we sacrifice our happiness and enjoyment of life by scrounging, never eating enough food, never driving because we'd be using oil products, and sitting in the dark so as not to use electricity? I think not.

The use of the world's resources is a moral issue. I recommend a balance between our needs, those of our contemporaries, and those of the generations who will follow us. Are there enough resources on this earth? Probably, if we don't waste what we have, and if innovation and technology continue to develop as they have in the past.

> **Remember**
> Environmental concerns are moral issues.

The Dangers in Predicting the Future

1. As technology has evolved, presumably limited resources have become more plentiful than we had thought. In the 1970s, the Club of Rome, a global think tank, predicted mass starvation as the population grew faster than the world's ability to feed itself. Club members, however, could not know about the advances in crop biology that were to occur, and the development of high yield grains and better fertilizers. The earth can provide plenty of food if we don't waste what we have.

2. Similarly, every ten years or so, some seemingly intelligent people predict that the earth will soon run out of oil. And almost like clockwork, a few years later, new oil fields are found or new techniques for extracting it are developed. There seems to be plenty of oil available, enough for our successors and us, if we don't waste it. And by the time in the distant future that the oil does indeed run out, as it eventually will, many substitutes for it will have been discovered. I could go on, but I think you get the idea. It's summarized in the adage, "Waste not, want not," the title of this chapter.

Be a Cheapskate

Forty or fifty years ago, a non-wasteful way of life would have been described by some people as "cheap," and a person who did not engage in wasteful activities might be labeled a "cheapskate." This was the era of "conspicuous consumption" and "keeping up with the Joneses," and to be thrifty or frugal was considered by some folks to be déclassé.

But then the environmental movement took hold, and suddenly, conserving was considered a virtue. It was considered politically correct to be "green," and many people switched their thinking about consumption and over-consumption. Now, it's cool to be concerned with the environment. Some movie stars, our American idols, buy hybrid vehicles to reduce gasoline consumption. There has been a sea change in people's attitudes. In fact, in the summer of 2008, the *Wall Street Journal* began a weekly column called "Cheapskate".

A "waste not, want not" approach to consumption not only makes your financial situation better by limiting your expenses, but also protects the earth and its inhabitants. It's a good way to live.

CHAPTER SIX
CREDIT CARDS AND DEBT

Getting out of debt, being out of debt, and staying out of debt are key features in a financially successful life. In this chapter we learn about debt, good and bad, and especially about credit cards and how they can be abused. As we learn about the ins and outs of debt and credit cards, I need to make clear that debt is not necessarily bad. Debt can be good or bad depending upon its purpose and its cost. If used carefully, debt can be helpful to achieving financial success.

Before discussing good and bad uses of debt, let's develop a context in which this is all happening.

Debt in the USA
We are a debtor nation in three ways:
1. Our federal government has run up a public debt of trillions of dollars resulting from years of deficit spending. It doesn't set a very good example for its citizens.
2. As I write, there is a financial meltdown taking place on Wall Street. Its primary cause is the excessive leverage caused by huge amounts of interconnected debt. The debt is now unraveling, or as they say on Wall Street, decoupling, and the end is not yet in sight.
3. Many Americans are up to their ears in debt. They live in a world of plastic, and charge consumer goods with abandon.

How Bad Is It?
U.S. News and World Report[1] informs us that, excluding mortgage debt, the average American with a credit file has $16,635 in debt. Additionally, the savings rate for these people is close to zero.

---

1   August 18-25, 2008

Sooner or later, this debt has to be paid off, governmental and consumer debt both. Governmental debt is the responsibility of all of us. What we don't pay off, our children and grandchildren will.

Some National Debt is Necessary
Governments, like businesses, need to have debt from time to time to meet their cash flow needs for operations and for capital investments. In good economic times, our federal government should use the excess revenues it collects to pay off part of the national debt. In bad times, it sometimes has to incur additional debt to help in an economic recovery. That's the way governments should use fiscal and monetary policy to control the economy. And when they do, things often work out well. But more often than not, governments issue debt in bad times, and when times get better, and they have more revenue with which to pay off the debt previously incurred, they increase their spending, just adding further to the debt. Governments can often get away with that because they have the power to tax and, in addition, the federal government can print money. But for us, as consumers and households, it's a different story.

Good Debt and Bad Debt
As consumers, we sometimes need to incur debt as we live our lives. There's nothing wrong with this if we handle it carefully. I believe that there is good debt and bad debt.

Good Debt
Good debt is used to make needed capital purchases, or for investing in the future. Some examples are:
- purchasing a residence
- purchasing a car
- getting a post-secondary education

These are items that have great utilitarian value. After all, most people need to live somewhere and have got to be able to drive around. And mortgage loan debt used to purchase a primary residence has the added advantage of allowing an itemized deduction of interest and property taxes on your federal tax return. This has the effect of reducing the net cost of the mortgage loan. And a post-secondary education is an investment that usually has a large payout over a person's lifetime.

Sometimes Personal Debt Is Necessary

For example, buying a house involves making an investment in real estate while providing a home for you and your family. Few people have the financial wherewithal to pay several hundred thousand dollars in cash to buy a house, so considering the advantages – personal and financial – of owning a house, taking out a mortgage loan makes a lot of sense. Monthly payments of principal and interest will pay back that debt over a period of 15 to 30 years, and you will own your house free and clear. These monthly payments often include taxes and insurance, so if you take out a mortgage loan, keep these items in mind when budgeting for the payments.

Generally, a mortgage loan[2] is good debt.

Some Debt Can Be Avoided Altogether

If you have not yet established a Rainy Day/Capital Expense fund (presented later in this chapter) that would allow you to pay cash for your car, taking out a car loan may be the only way you can have a car with which to get around. Monthly payments of principal and interest on a car loan are usually paid over a period of three to five years. A car loan may be considered good debt in these circumstances.

Generally speaking, a mortgage loan on a primary residence represents an appreciating asset and a car loan represents a depreciating asset. In other words, while you are using them, homes generally increase in value, while the value of automo-

---

2   I refer here to a first mortgage loan. Increasing your cash flow by taking out additional mortgage loans, commonly known as home equity loans or second mortgages, is a dangerous activity that has led to the insolvency of thousands of households thus far in the 21st Century.

biles decreases. They are hard assets that you are paying for over the lives of the assets themselves. And the assets themselves provide collateral for the loans taken against them, so the interest rate charged is generally not burdensome.

Educational Debt As an Investment

And finally, there is debt incurred for a college education. Approximately two-thirds of college graduates have borrowed money through student loans to pay for their education. Education is a worthwhile endeavor for many reasons, not the least of which is that it can prepare you for a better paying job There is nothing wrong with this debt. But, it must be paid back.

Most college graduates with loans took out Stafford or Perkins loans. These loans may be paid off in a variety of ways, and often over a period of many years. There are grace periods, deferments, forbearances, and forgiveness provisions available. Details are offered on the Student Loan Marketing Association (Sallie Mae) website, **www.salliemae.com**.

Student Loans

Because these student loans generally have interest rates lower than credit cards, and because if you are late in your payments, SallieMae will not hound you the way other creditors would, some graduates neglect to pay attention to the payment schedules. This is a risky business, and can cause your loan to go into default. This can affect your ability to get another student loan, and will show up on your credit report for seven years. During this time, you may have trouble getting a mortgage or other loan, and it might even interfere with your ability to rent an apartment. So, plan to pay this debt off in a timely manner.

Notwithstanding the potential problems in repaying these debts, incurring debt for these reasons is fine. This is good debt. On the other hand, there's bad debt.

Bad Debt

Bad debt is made up of two kinds of debt:

1. Debt incurred to purchase non-essential items such as vacations, extensive wardrobes, gourmet meals, cruises, etc., when you can't afford them.
2. Debt that carries a high interest rate. Among the worst kind of debt is credit card debt (e.g., Visa or MasterCard), and department store debt. Interest rates on this kind of debt are sometimes as high as 29% annually.

The Trap of Making Minimum Payments

Some people with this kind of debt never pay it off, but rather make minimum payments month after month, year after year, with barely any reduction in principal. This is <u>not</u> a good use of debt. This is <u>not</u> the way to accumulate wealth. It's the way to poverty, or at least the way to decreased wealth. Recall our discussion in Chapter Four of Rent-to-Own purchasing. By the time you've made your final payment, you've paid for the item several times over.

My philosophy is to use debt only when it is to your advantage, and not to the bank's advantage. Credit cards are best used as a convenience for purchasing consumer goods or for emergency situations, and not as a way of forestalling payment.

Credit Cards

Banks really like me. They send me offers to affiliate with them and to take advantage of their credit lines. Every week or so, I get another solicitation, even from banks I've never heard of. I throw them all away. The issuers of my two existing credit cards often send me checks to write for additional money, which will, of course, appear as charges on my monthly statement. I throw these out, too.

If you are a recent college graduate, no doubt you have already been inundated with solicitations from banks. Should you have credit cards and use them? Yes, but only if you know the terms of your agreement with the bank, and only if you have the discipline to pay off your entire balance each month.

How Many Do You Need?
I have only two cards. I find that sufficient for my needs. Besides, I don't want all that mail offering me ways to incur more debt, and I don't want to have to keep track of all those cards.

One card I've had for 40 years and the other for 10 years, I'm glad I have them. It makes purchasing things online and in person much easier. Indeed, at most car rental counters, they won't take cash. You must have a credit or debit card. So, credit cards can be a great thing to have, if used correctly. In this chapter, I will present some ideas on how to use credit cards and how not to use them.

But first: a warning on the misuse and abuse of credit cards.

In the 1967 classic movie, *The Graduate*, at a party celebrating Benjamin's (played by Dustin Hoffman) graduation from college, a family friend pulled Benjamin to the side and told him that there was one word he should think about when planning his career: "Plastics." At that time, that was good advice for planning a business.

If you were to ask me what's the most frequent source of financial worries many young couples have, I'd give the same answer, "Plastics." But I would be referring to credit cards.

Plastic Cards are Not Money
Every so often, I tune in to a radio or TV broadcast where a financial advisor is receiving calls from listeners or viewers. Many of these people are in serious financial trouble. And virtually every one of them has credit card debt that is overwhelming them, sometimes to the point of wanting to declare personal

bankruptcy. It's sad to hear these stories, because with some basic knowledge and some discipline, they probably could have avoided falling into the credit card trap.

Types of Plastic Cards

Let's start with the basics about "plastics." There are several types of cards in this category:

- Credit cards issued by banks
- Debit cards
- Automatic Teller Machine (ATM) cards
- Charge cards
- Store cards

> ## Be careful
> Used well, credit cards are a blessing. Used poorly, they are a curse.

And let's continue with a basic truth: When you borrow money from someone or something, you have to pay it back, and with interest. There is no such thing as a free lunch from a stranger. Money charged to a credit card is, in essence, a loan. Banks lend you money in order to make money for themselves. As my grandmother might have said, "They're not in business for their health."

Bank-Issued Credit Cards (Visa, MasterCard, etc.)

Banks offering you credit cards make money several ways. First, they may charge you an annual fee for just having the account. Then, every time you charge something, the merchant is charged a small amount that goes into the banks' coffers. Actually, you are paying that small amount, because the cost of the merchant's charge is built into the price you pay.[3] Then, on a monthly basis, you have to pay the amounts you charged. If you do not pay off your monthly balance, the bank will charge you interest as high as 29% in some cases. Of course, if your payment is late, or the balance exceeds your credit limit on the card, additional fees will be assessed. This is a very lucrative business for them.

---

3   This is evidenced by many gas stations that charge one price for customers paying in cash, and a higher price for those paying with plastic.

Different banks have different policies for credit card holders. Some charge an annual fee, and some don't. Some have higher interest rates, and some have lower rates. Some have due dates at the end of the month, some have earlier due dates. Some give rewards, and some don't.

Unpaid Balance Problems

If you have charges on your card, banks will allow you to pay a certain minimum each month. Indeed, they may not just allow this, but they probably will actively encourage it. Of course, you'll be paying interest on the unpaid balance. That's very beneficial to them, but it can be a disaster for you. Depending upon the minimum payment required, the amount of principal being paid on, and the interest rate you are paying, it can take a decade or more to pay off your account. And then, when you compare the original principal of your debt with the amount of interest you paid, you will have paid the principal many times over before the debt is paid off.

Debit Cards

Credit cards and debit cards look alike and, in some respects, are alike. They are both plastic and they both are alternatives to paying cash. Some banks issue cards that may be used inter-changeably as a debit or a credit card, or even as an ATM card, as described below.

A debit card is associated with your checking account. Typically, when you make a purchase, it immediately debits (sub-tracts from) your account for the amount of the purchase. Most banks will have an overdraft provision, which takes effect when you make a purchase that exceeds your bank balance. They will allow you to do this up to a certain maximum, usually $500, but they will assess a service charge to your account of $25-$50 for each transaction that exceeds your bank balance. If you max out on your overdraft margin, your account will not allow a debit to be made, and your transaction cannot be completed.

ATM Cards
These cards will allow you to receive cash from your account. You are not borrowing anything. You are merely tapping the resources in your checking or savings account. They are really another form of a debit card. The money is coming from your account, but rather than going directly to the vendor, it is going to you in the form of greenbacks.

Charge Cards (e.g. AMEX or Diners Club)
These also allow purchasing without using cash, but they don't extend credit. They allow you to charge purchases, and you are expected to pay off the charges when the issuing company sends you your monthly statement. These cards generally have annual fees, and are considered by some folks to be more chic than bankcards. The distinctions between these cards and credit cards are getting somewhat blurry because American Express, the largest issuer of charge cards, now offers a credit card as well as a charge card.

Store Cards (e.g., Macy's or Target)
Many stores, especially national chains, issue their own credit cards, offering what they call "revolving credit." They often offer you incentives, such as 10% off your first purchase with the card, to sign you up for their cards so you will be inclined to do your shopping in their stores. Their interest charges are not low. Generally they range from a 15% to 25% annualized percentage rate.

All of these cards allow you to make a purchase without paying immediately with cash. For the sake of simplicity, I'll refer to them collectively as "credit cards."

The Meaning of "Cash"
When I use the word *cash*, I am referring to greenbacks (dollar bills) or bank checks. If I mean greenbacks, but not checks, I'll use the word greenbacks.

How to Use Credit Cards

Here are some simple rules for the appropriate use of credit cards:

- Read the fine print on any application for a credit card in which you might be interested. It's called fine print because the print type is quite small, uninviting, and not reader-friendly. Perhaps another reason it's called fine print is because it's fine for the bank if you don't read it or understand it. You might be surprised to find out some of the details revealed in the fine print.[4] You need to know what you're getting into when you sign up for a card.
- Select a credit card that has no annual fee, a reasonable interest rate (just in case the payment doesn't get to them on time), a grace period of at least two weeks (from the time of your last purchase to the due date for payment), and a card that doesn't hit you with surprises, extra fees, or frequent changes in interest rates. If you can get a card that has some extra bonuses, such as free gifts or cash back, so much the better. You can compare the many features of different credit cards at **www.creditcards.com**.
- Make purchases on items that are needs and reasonable wants. No exceptions.
- Make charges on the card as if you were paying cash – carefully and prudently. Many people buy more and pay more when using plastic, compared to using cash. They are less aware of spending. Don't fall into that trap.
- When the monthly statement arrives, write out your check for the entire amount and mail it in a timely manner.

---

4   For example, many credit card issuers include a "universal default clause." This means that if you pay <u>any</u> bill (e.g. an electric bill, or a phone bill) late, you are subject to an increase in the interest rate charged on your credit card. This applies even if you have paid your credit card bill on time.

- Don't get cash advances from your credit card. There is no grace period for such transactions. This means that the cash advance is subject to interest charges as of the date of the advance. This is an expensive loan to take out.

These rules will not make the issuing banks very happy. However, these rules are written for your benefit, not theirs. When you use your credit card in this way, you are using it for your convenience, not as a way to spend money you don't have. **If you cannot or will not pay off your monthly charges at the end of the billing period, then take a hefty pair of scissors, cut your cards into pieces and discard them. Pay cash for everything.**

Oops. I Already Have Credit Card Debt.

Perhaps this book is coming to you when you've already incurred some credit card debt. What should you do?

- The first thing to do when you've dug yourself into a hole and want to get out is to stop digging. If you have several credit cards, cut them all up except one. Make no more charges on this card except when absolutely necessary (for instance, if a vendor won't take cash).
- Pay cash for everything. If you don't have the cash, then don't make the purchase. Defer it until you have the cash.
- Draw up a schedule that lists your credit card debts in order from the highest to the lowest interest rate charged. Then, pay the minimum amounts on all but the first one on the list. For that one, the one having the highest interest, pay off as much as you can. When that one is paid off, start paying off the card with the next highest interest rate. Continue this until all the debt is gone.
- Look over your balance sheet. Are there any assets you can do without? Sell something of value, and use the cash to pay off some of the debt.

- In your budget, include an item for rapid and systematic payoff of your debt.
- If you are swamped with debt, contact the finance company and see if they can change the terms of your debt, or help in some other way.

As stated earlier, if you have debt, the first thing to do to achieve financial success is to pay it off. Bit by bit, as long as it takes, rid yourself of this burden and then you'll be at square one. If you are already at square one, then so much the better. Let's assume you are there – that is, debt free.

Be Your Own Banker

If you ever want to get ahead of the game and be a financial success, you have to avoid, as much as possible, paying interest on debt. You don't achieve financial success by paying people interest. Rather, you achieve financial success by having other people pay you interest. And how do you do that? Simple. You have to become your own banker. And what does that mean? It means that when you need to spend money, you borrow it from yourself, and not from someone else. You need to develop a **Rainy Day/Capital Expense (RD/CE) Fund**, as presented below. Let me explain.

To be your own banker, you need some capital, a reserve of money you can tap into when necessary. You develop this by living with your means, and saving/investing the remainder. In other words, budget and spend in order to have a positive cash flow.

You've read Chapters Four and Five, you have some ideas on how to get value for the things you purchase, and you know how to avoid waste. From following these recommendations and living within your means, your income and spending patterns will allow you to have a positive cash flow.

> **A Smart Hobby**
> Having ready cash lets you be your own banker.

Rainy Day/Capital Expense Fund (RD/CE)

Establish your RD/CE Fund, perhaps initially in an interest bearing savings account, and every month put some money into it. Perhaps it can only be $100. Do it. Perhaps it can be $500 or more. Do it.

Pay yourself first. Discipline yourself to make regular monthly payments to this fund so it grows into $15,000 to $30,000. It may take some time, but having this fund is necessary to financial success.

RD/CE Fund for Two Purposes

What you want to have is a chunk of change at your disposal, to use for two and only two purposes:

- To fund an emergency, with money you can tap if you lose your job, or if you have a medical emergency of some sort.
- To fund a major expenditure, such as a car, a new roof on your house, a replacement washing machine, etc.

Although you cannot know what (if any) emergencies might occur, you probably can predict what some major expenses might be: a car, an appliance, etc. What can be predicted should be written down, and budgetary provision in your RD/CE fund should be made for those expenditures.

Difficult, But Not Impossible

Of all the ideas in this book, the establishment of an RD/CE fund may be the most difficult to implement, because it requires a discipline that is uncommon in our debt-oriented society and it may be something you've never done before. Perhaps your parents have never done this before. Perhaps you don't know of anyone your age, or of any age, who takes this approach of saving and spending. That's understandable.

The idea of deferred gratification is just not a part of our culture.

Many people earn and spend, living hand-to-mouth, from pay-check to paycheck. Financial institutions and the media portray buying on credit and paying over time as a standard, accepted way of living, and it's tough to buck a trend. But it can and should be done, if you want to be financially successful.

Pay with Cash
If you have this RD/CE fund and you need to make a major pur-chase, like a car, take the money out of the fund and buy the car with cash. You will incur no debt this way and will not have to make monthly payments, as you might have previously done. Also, very often you can get a better price on your car by paying cash. I frequently see advertisements for cars that read some-thing like, "0% financing, or $3,000 cash back." Skip the financ-ing and take the cash.

Replenish the Fund
After paying cash for your car, replenish the money withdrawn from this fund, by continuing to make your monthly payments to the RD/CE fund. Instead of making monthly payments to a lending agency to pay off a car loan, you are making monthly payments to yourself, thus replacing the money withdrawn to make the purchase. You are not paying interest to a bank. The bank, where your money is located, is paying interest to you on your RD/CE Fund's balance. You are your own banker. You've borrowed from yourself and you have paid yourself back. This is a good way to live. Buy something with cash and it's yours. Buy something on credit and it's not yours until the loan is paid off. I prefer the first way.

Be Careful with This Fund
I mentioned above that this fund has two and only two pur-poses: to fund an emergency or make a capital purchase. If you are going to save money in the RD/CE Fund and then blow it on a vacation, you've missed the point. Perhaps you want to have a special fund for a vacation, but budget for that separately. Leave the RD/CE Fund for the two purposes mentioned earlier.

Credit Reports

When you have used credit from various business entities, the way you have handled your debt is reported to credit bureaus. The three major bureaus are TransUnion, Equifax, and Experian. Potential lenders, such as banks, and others who have a stake in your ability to pay your obligations, such as landlords from whom you seek to rent an apartment, will probably contact these credit bureaus asking for a credit report on you.

What's In It?

A credit report contains personal information about you, and information about every credit account you have. There is information about the punctuality of your payments, your account balances, and credit limits. In addition, there may be a running record of problems you may have had in paying money you owed people, such as evictions from apartments, unpaid traffic tickets, bankruptcies, unpaid alimony or child support payments, bounced checks, etc.

Credit problems can stay on your credit report for a long time. If you were to file for bankruptcy, it could take as long as 10 years before the stigma is erased.

What's Its Purpose?

A credit report reveals to potential lenders information about your character, your capacity for debt, and your financial and personal stability. In short, the report shows just how credit-worthy you are.

An analysis of your personal and financial situation is summarized in a credit score, which usually ranges from 300 to 850. The higher the score, the more credit-worthy you are. Scores from
- 700 to 850 are excellent
- 680 to 699 are good
- 620 to 679 are okay

Scores below 620 may make it difficult for you to get credit. Or if you do get it, it may come at a higher rate than someone with a higher score.

How Can I Find Out My Score?

By the provisions of the Fair and Accurate Credit Transactions Act (FACT Act), you are entitled to a free credit report from each of the three credit bureaus listed above, every 12 months. You can access your credit reports on the Web at **www.annualcreditreport.com**.

Credit Insurance

Sometimes when you buy an item on credit, such as a house or a refrigerator, the salesperson will try to sell you life or disability insurance to cover your debt in case you are unable to pay it.[5] Generally, life or disability insurance tied to one item is an expensive way to go. You'll get more coverage at a lower premium cost with a more general life or disability policy. This will be presented in Chapter Ten.

Personal Bankruptcy

Under current law, there are two possibilities for dealing with personal bankruptcy – Chapter 7 and Chapter 13.

- In Chapter 7 bankruptcy, the debtor's assets (with a few exemptions) are liquidated, and the cash generated from the liquidation is used to pay off the creditors.
- In Chapter 13 bankruptcy, the debtor develops a three- to five-year plan to pay down the unsecured debt.

In either of these cases, the bankruptcy event will be a part of the debtor's credit report.

---

5   If your credit is really bad, the salesperson may insist on you having such a policy so as to secure the loan. If so, try shopping somewhere else.

Alternatives to Bankruptcy

Personal bankruptcy should be considered a last resort, to be used only after all the alternatives have been exhausted. There are three viable alternatives:

1. Out-of-court settlement with creditors – In this procedure, the debtor talks with each individual creditor to work out some sort of arrangement to settle the outstanding debt. Perhaps one of the following might be done:
- The interest rate could be lowered
- The time in which to pay the debt could be lengthened
- Some of the debt could be forgiven

2. Debt Counseling – The debtor gets help from a person who is experienced and knowledgeable in personal finance. The National Foundation for Credit Counseling (NFCC) is a non-profit organization with agencies and offices countrywide. Their web-site is **www.nfcc.org**.

3. Debt Consolidation Loan – In this alternative, if a debtor owns a house or any other asset with substantial equity in it, the debtor can take out an equity loan and use the cash to pay off creditors. Frequently, the interest rate on secured loans, such as these, is much lower than the rates on unsecured debt, such as credit cards and store cards.

These alternatives are often employed in conjunction with one another, in order to deal with high debt loads. Nevertheless, some folks have so much debt that their situation is hopeless and bankruptcy is the only solution.

A Word of Caution

Bankruptcy is a messy procedure to go through. It gives you a bad reputation in the credit world and can lead to a diminished sense of self-worth. The best way to deal with it is to avoid it in the first place. This can be done by following the recommendations found in this book, by being prudent, and conducting your financial life in such a way as to preclude financial problems.

There is more information about bankruptcy available to you on the Internet at this web site: **www.bankruptcyinformation.com**.

Fast Money Schemes to Avoid

There are many businesses that profit from a debtor's need for fast cash. These should be avoided.

- *Credit "Repair" Companies* – Some companies may offer to take all your loans, consolidate them, and then you make one payment directly to the company. Sounds like a good deal, and you won't have creditors calling you at all hours of the day and night. However, you may be sure that these folks aren't doing this for nothing. Be sure to find out what their fees are for this service. Then figure out if you'd really benefit from such an arrangement.
- *Car Title Loans* – In this arrangement, you turn over the title of your car as collateral for an immediate cash loan. When you pay the loan company back, you'll get your title back. Of course, you'll be paying a hefty interest rate for this convenience. And if you don't pay the loan back, you can kiss your car goodbye.
- *Payday Loans* – Some companies will lend you money until you get your next paycheck. Typically, it works like this. Let's say you give them a check for $500, drawn on your checking account, and they immediately give you a $450 check, which you cash. They hold your check for two weeks until your paycheck is deposited in your checking account, at which time they cash your check. You borrowed $450 for two weeks, and you paid them back $500. The $50 difference you paid, the price for the two-week loan, represents an 11.11% interest rate. In annual terms, the interest you paid was 289%.

Credit is Good

It is said that credit is "the oil that lubricates our economy."

I agree. And as I write these words, the American (as well as the world's) economy is in dire circumstances because of the abuse of credit by our financial institutions. The federal government is pumping hundreds of billions of dollars to resolve the problem. This is because without credit, our economy will cease to function.

At a personal finance level, credit is an important tool to be used, but only in a careful, deliberate, and prudent way. If misused, it can cause you trouble. And there are many predatory firms out there who claim to want to offer you a helping hand, but do not have your best interests at heart.

Nevertheless, if used wisely, credit will enhance your chances for financial success.

CHAPTER SEVEN
PLANNING YOUR RETIREMENT

As you come to this chapter, you might be thinking, "Retirement? What? I just started working. Do I need to start planning for it now?" The answer is yes, although you do not need to put much money into retirement planning right now. The key issue is time, as we will see in Chapter Nine.

At retirement, your income will probably come from one or more of these sources:
- Your retirement account(s) from your employment
- Social Security
- Your supplemental retirement accounts you funded alone
- Other funds not necessarily earmarked for retirement, but used for such

Before we begin the explanation of these funding sources, there is a basic concept you must understand. This is *compound interest*, and over time, it's the most important financial friend you'll have.

Time is your Ally
Albert Einstein is reported to have said, "The most powerful force in the universe is compound interest." It certainly is powerful. It gets its power from adding interest to the principal, and then computing interest on the new, larger principal, and continuing to do so.

A Penny is a Powerful Tool
Think about this: If you had invested one cent in the mid-first century, and that one cent was compounded at the modest rate of 4% annually, you'd be the richest person on earth. Yes, richer than Bill Gates and Warren Buffett combined. In fact, you'd have

approximately $1.165946 to the 32nd power. That's 1,165,946 trillion trillion dollars (give or take a few trillion dollars due to rounding errors), and that's probably more than all the money in the world.

How could this happen?
By year 100, the $0.01 would have grown to $0.51. By year 300, its value would be $1,288.25. By year 700 it would have grown to $8,381,804,155. My calculator had to go into scientific notation at year 800 with a balance of $4.233 to the 11th power.

The Magic of Compounding
The example of one penny invested making you the richest person on earth shows the magic of compounding. But compounding needs time to do its work, as just seen. Here are some examples more in keeping with a reasonable life expectancy. All examples assume payments made at the beginning of each month, monthly compounding, and a 6% annual interest rate.

Take a look at Table 7-1. This shows the results of making monthly investments of $100 with compounding at the rate of 6%. The first column shows the number of years in which these monthly investments compounded. The second column shows the total amount invested in that period. The third column shows the value of that amount at the end of the period.

Table 7-1 Results of $100 Monthly Investments Compounded at 6%		
YEARS OF COMPOUNDING	TOTAL INVESTED	VALUE AT END OF PERIOD
20	$24,000	$46,204
30	$36,000	$100,450
40	$48,000	$199,149

Small Amounts But Big Results

As you can see from Table 7-1, in 20 years you would have contributed $24,000, which would have grown to $46,204 at the end of the 20 years. Similar data are shown for 30 and 40 years. But note carefully in Table 7-2, the ratios of years of compounding to the values at the end of the period. There is a 50% increase in the amount of money and time involved in the investment. But the value of the investment at the ends of these periods increases from $46,204 to $100,450, representing an increase of 117%.

Table 7-2
Percentage Increase of Years of Compounding and Values at the End of the Period

			INCREASE
YEARS OF COMPOUNDING	20	30	50%
TOTAL INVESTED	$2,400	$3,600	50%
VALUE AT END OF PERIOD	$46,204	$100,450	117%

Even more dramatic is the increase from 20 years to 40 years of compounding, as shown in Table 7-3. There is a 100% increase in the amount of money and time involved in the investment. But the value of the investment at the ends of these periods, from $46,204 to $199,149, represents an increase of 331%.

Table 7-3
Percentage Increase of Years of Compounding and Values at the End of the Period

			INCREASE
YEARS OF COMPOUNDING	20	40	100%
TOTAL INVESTED	$2,400	$4,800	100%
VALUE AT END OF PERIOD	$46,204	$199,149	331%

Tables 7-4 and 7-5 show similar data for monthly contributions of $300 and $500 respectively. The ratios of years of compounding to values at the end of the period are the same. The

Table 7-4
Results of $300 Monthly Contributions
Compounded at 6%

YEARS OF COMPOUNDING	TOTAL INVESTED	VALUE AT END OF PERIOD
20	$72,000	$138,612
30	108,000	301,355
40	144,000	597,447

Table 7-5
Results of $500 Monthly Contributions
Compounded at 6%

YEARS OF COMPOUNDING	TOTAL INVESTED	VALUE AT END OF PERIOD
20	$120,000	$231,020
30	186,000	502,258
40	240,000	995,745

amounts, of course, are larger, because the amounts invested are larger.

You can calculate the results of varied amounts of money, time, and interest at **www.econedlink.org**.

Time is the Best Friend You Can Have

Now take a look at Table 7-6. This table extracts data from Tables 7-1 and 7-2 and shows how time is your ally.

Table 7-6 shows that $100 per month, compounding for 40 years, results in $199,149, more value than the $138,612 that results from $300 per month compounding for 20 years. Thus,

Table 7-6
Comparison of Two Investment Strategies

MONTHLY INVESTMENT	YEARS OF COMPOUNDING	TOTAL AMOUNT INVESTED	VALUE AT END OF PERIOD
$100	40	$24,000	$199,149
$300	20	$72,000	$138,612

you can sometimes do better putting in less money earlier than more money later. In other words, a part of your financial success is not just a question of how <u>much</u> you invested; it's how <u>early</u> you start investing.

A Word of Caution
It should be noted that the examples shown in the tables above represent hypothetical scenarios. Variations in earnings rates, taxes, and inflation have not been factored in. In reality, the values at the end of the period would vary somewhat from the figures presented, and of course, the purchasing power of those figures would be diminished by even a slow rate of inflation. Notwithstanding these factors, continuous compounding is a strong and useful tool in accumulating wealth.

Compounding and The Rule of 72
This is a rule you ought to know. There is an easy way to find out how to double your money. There are two factors:
- the interest rate
- the time of compounding

Any combination of these two factors that yields a product of 72 will tell you how to double your money. Or stated otherwise, when 72 is divided by either of these factors, the result will be the other factor.

If You Know the Interest Rate...
At an interest rate of 8%, how long will it take for the money to double?

72/8% = 9, so it will take nine years at 8% to double your money.

If You Know the Number of Years...
What interest rate do you need for your money to double in 6 years?

72/6 years = 12, so you need an interest rate of 12% to double your money in six years.

Retirement Accounts from Employment

There are two major types of retirement benefits sponsored by employers: defined benefit programs and defined contribution programs.

Defined Benefit Plans

Years ago, many employers provided pension benefits for their employees. The employee made a contribution, the employer made a contribution, and the money went into a pension fund. At retirement, a formula was applied which used three factors:

- number of years of service
- average salary of last several years
- a given percentage

These factors were multiplied together, and the product was a defined annual pension that would be paid to the employee in monthly installments for the rest of his or her life. For example, Employee Jake worked for Acme Steel for 32 years, his average salary for the last five years was $75,000 and the percentage applied was 1½ %. Multiplying the factors, 32 years times $75,000 times 1.5%, yields an annual benefit of $36,000, probably paid in monthly checks of $3,000.[1]

If It's Offered, Be Happy

If your employer sponsors a defined benefit program, you will probably have no choice as to your participation. You're in it. Your contributions are pooled with those of others, and after a period of years – perhaps ten or so – you will be "vested." This means that you can leave the funds with the pension fund even if you no longer work for that employer, and when you get to a certain age, usually 65, benefits will be paid to you. If you leave before the vesting period, your contributions, but not those of

---

1   Plans vary as to what constitutes years of service, how many years of salary go into computation of an average salary, and the specific percentage applied.

your employer, may be returned to you. Typically, you have no control as to what the pension funds are invested in.

These defined benefit plans are sometimes called "old-fashioned pensions." Many state and municipal employees are covered by such pension plans. However, many private companies have phased them out (if they ever had them), and instead offer defined contribution plans.

Defined Contribution Plans (401(k) Plans)

The most frequently encountered defined contribution plans are known as 401(k) plans, named after the section of the tax code where they appear. In these plans, the employees make contributions representing a percentage of their salaries, perhaps 6%. Employers make a matching contribution, usually about half of the employees', but sometimes more.[2] The money goes into any of several possible investment vehicles under the supervision of a fiduciary institution.

If It's Offered, Take It

If your employer offers a defined contribution program, you should participate in it. This is especially true if the employer offers a matching contribution. For example, if you contribute $1,000 and your employer will match half of that, $500, this $500 represents a 100% yield on the first $500 of your contribution. That kind of return is hard to get anywhere and it's free – that is, there's no risk on your part.

403(b) Plans

Some employees who work for non-profit companies, such as hospitals and schools, are eligible for 403(b) plans, which work similarly to 401(k) plans. These are often the primary retirement plans for them. However, some state and municipal employees who are participants in their defined benefit programs may also have a supplemental 403(b) plan to enhance their retirement

---

2   In these plans, as with defined benefit plans, the details will vary from employer to employer.

income. This supplemental plan is typically funded with only the employee's money, and not the employers.

Earnings on 401(k) and 403(b) accounts are tax-deferred, which means that the earnings can compound at a faster rate than if they were taxed annually. Generally, they are a good deal for you.

What To Invest In
Often, the employee has a choice of which particular investments the money is put in. If you have a choice as to what asset types your account is invested in, choose a combination of 65% stock index funds, 20% international funds, and 15% bond funds. The characteristics of these funds will be discussed in later chapters. As you get closer to retirement, you might change these percentages to be somewhat more conservative. At retirement, the money in the employee's account may be withdrawn in a lump sum, or may be annuitized, thus yielding a monthly income.

Employer's Corporate Stock
Some corporations will make contributions to their employees' retirement plans with stock in the corporation. If that is your only choice, take it. It's free. But bear in mind that if that stock is the only security in your retirement plan, you are sitting on a non-diversified portfolio, and this is dangerous. Should the company get into financial trouble, the value of your stock could be severely impacted in a negative way (think Enron here). And on top of that, you might lose your job, a double whammy.

Need for Diversification
Some corporations will give their stock to employees' retirement systems, and then require the stock to be held for a certain period of time before it can be sold. If that is the case, then hold the stock, and when the mandatory holding period is over, consider whether you should continue to hold it. Even if the company is a good one and you would like to retain ownership of

your shares, bear in mind that your retirement fund lacks diversity. I'd recommend that you sell at least a portion of the stock, and reinvest the proceeds in other financial instruments. It's not good to take chances with your retirement funds.

Social Security

Many employees, both in the public and private sectors, are covered by Social Security. This program was started during the Great Depression, and was aimed at providing some funds for retirees through a payroll deduction from those who are currently working. Presently, you pay 6.2% of your salary up to a wage base ($102,000 for 2008). Your employer pays the same amount.[3] This goes into a "trust fund."

Will It Be There for You?

The Social Security program presents a dilemma for young folks like you. It is not now, nor was it ever, a financially sound program. And notwithstanding the "trust fund" idea, there are not sufficient funds to provide currently promised benefits for all future retirees. Furthermore, you have no property rights to your anticipated Social Security benefit.

Congress created the program in 1935. They have changed it many, many times, and could (and probably will) change it again. You might get some benefits, and then again you might not. But the benefits that you might get will probably not be as generous as the benefits retirees are receiving now.

Supplemental Retirement Accounts

Regardless of whether you have an employer-sponsored retirement account, you may choose to have an Individual Retirement Account (IRA). Congress legislated IRAs in the early 1980s to encourage workers to take some personal responsibility for their retirement. Earnings in an IRA are tax-deferred until with-

---

3   An additional 1.45% for Medicare is also paid by you, with your employer kicking in a similar amount. Currently, there is no wage base cap on this, though.

drawal. If you have a Roth IRA, the earnings in your account are tax-exempt, that is, you pay no taxes on any withdrawal after age 59 ½. There are income limits for starting a Roth IRA. For 2008, the income limits are $166,000 for a married couple, and $114,000 for a single person. If you earn more than this, you are not eligible for a Roth IRA, but you still can contribute to a traditional IRA.

Tax Deferral or Avoidance

When Uncle Sam gives you a gift, open it, rejoice, and be glad in it. He gave us the opportunity to invest for our future retirement, and not pay taxes on the earnings while the money is accumulating, or in the case of a Roth IRA, never pay taxes on them. We should take advantage of this.

As a people, we Americans are taxed on our income at the federal level as well as sometimes at the state and local levels. These taxes are also applied to our investment income. Within recent memory, interest, dividends, and short-term capital gains[4] were taxed as regular income, subject to tax rates as high as 39.6%, while long-term capital gains[5] were taxed at rates as high as 20%. Beginning in 2001, tax rates on many investments have been reduced, but they still represent a diminution of returns on investments.

Congress Wants to Help You

Congress wants to encourage us to prepare financially for our retirement, so it has given us some gifts in the form of letting us defer, and sometimes even avoid entirely, the taxes which would normally be paid on the earnings from our investments. These gifts include employer-sponsored retirement plans like traditional pension plans (defined benefit) and 401(k) plans (defined contribution); Keogh and SEP-IRA plans for the self-employed; individual retirement accounts of many types, and 403(b) plans for some employees working in the non-profit area.

---

4   Gains of the sale of assets held for less than one year.
5   Gains on the sale of assets held for a year or more.

Tax-Free Compounding

Investment vehicles that allow tax-free compounding (i.e., tax payments deferred or avoided) are excellent opportunities for the enhanced accumulation of wealth. The differences between compounding in taxable accounts, contrasted to compounding in non-taxable accounts, are dramatic. For instance, assume you make payments of $100 at the beginning of every month to an account that yields a 6% return, and you are in the 30% marginal tax bracket. In a fully taxable account your balance in 20 years would be $37,513. However, in a non-taxable account, after 20 years your balance would be $46,204, a difference of $8,691, or 23% more.

Tax Advantaged Investments and Accounts

We should note at the outset of this section that most <u>investments</u> – stock, bonds, mutual funds, etc – are taxable at one rate or another. But if these investments are held in tax-advantaged <u>accounts</u>, the taxes on them may be deferred or avoided entirely. In other words, it's the account that is tax-advantaged, not the investment itself.[6]

Taxation Makes a Big Difference

Table 7-7 shows the results of making monthly investments of $100 for 20, 30, and 40 years, compounding monthly at a rate of 6%, when you are in a marginal tax bracket of 30%.

As you can see from Table 7-7, the benefits of investing in tax-deferred accounts rather than taxable accounts are enormous. That's why investing in 401(k)s, 403(b)s, IRAs, and other tax-deferred accounts makes a lot of sense.

Withdrawals from Tax-Favored Accounts

When Congress set up these tax-favored investment accounts – 401(k), 403(b), IRA, Roth IRA – they sought to encourage individuals to save for their retirement. Thus, there are rules that

---

6   An exception to this statement is an investment in a bond fund which contains state and municipal bonds which are not subject to federal taxation.

Table 7-7
Taxable vs. Tax-Deferred
Compounding of Earnings of $100 Invested Monthly

YEARS	TAXABLE	TAX DEFERRED	DOLLAR DIFFERENCE	PERCENT DIFFERENCE
20	$37,513	$46,204	$8,691	23%
30	$71,934	$100,452	$28,518	40%
40	$124,280	$199,149	$74,869	60%

govern premature withdrawals from these accounts. The rules are subject to change by Congress, or the Internal Revenue Service's interpretation, but here is the gist of the current rules.

There Might Be Penalties

For tax-deferred accounts, there is no penalty for taking withdrawals after age 59 ½. If you withdraw funds before that age, the withdrawal may be subject to a 10% penalty. In all these accounts except a Roth IRA, you <u>must</u> begin to take withdrawals at age 70 ½. The penalty for a late withdrawal is 50% of the required withdrawal.

For a 401(k) or a 403(b), if you take withdrawals before age 59 ½, this is considered an early withdrawal, and there are stringent rules to follow. If you have a bona fide hardship (as defined by the IRS), such as unreimbursed medical expenses or a disability, there will be no penalty assessed.

With an IRA, if you want to use the funds for the first-time purchase of a residence or for educational expenses, you may borrow the money for these purposes and there will be no penalty assessed.

More details about penalties on withdrawals can be found at **http:/beginnersinvest.about.com/cs/iras/aairafees htm**.

Another Penalty

To my way of thinking, perhaps the worst penalty for early withdrawal of these funds is the loss of the principal withdrawn and the loss of potential earnings on that principal. Thus, I discourage early withdrawals unless absolutely necessary.

The rules concerning these tax-favored retirement accounts are tricky and are subject to revision at any time. Before taking any action on withdrawing funds, you should talk to someone who understands the ins and outs of the current tax code.

Planning Supplemental Retirement Income

In the earlier part of this chapter, you saw the miraculous effects of compounding on a relatively small amount of money over a period of time. You can use this technique to develop a substantial addition to your retirement funding through systematic contributions to non-tax-advantaged accounts. Here's how this can happen:

Funding the Account

Let's say you're 30 years old and you plan to retire at age 65. So, you have 35 years of time for compounding until retirement. Further, you plan on living another 35 years until age 100. And let's say that you want to have a corpus of $300,000 to draw upon at the time of your retirement. And finally, let's assume that you'll be investing prudently, making regular monthly investments, and receive a return of 6% compounded monthly. Here's how it would play out.

As shown in Table 7-8, you would need to contribute $211 monthly, for an annual contribution of $2,532. Your total contribution over the 35 years would be $88,620. And now, at age 65, you have $300,000 to draw from.

You can calculate how much you'll need to save to achieve a financial goal on the Web at **http:/moneycentral.msn.com/home.asp**.

Table 7-8
Funding a Target Amount of $300,000 Over 35 Years

Monthly Payments	$211
Annualized	$2,532
Total Paid In Over 35 Years	$88,620
Value of Account After 35 Years	$300,000

Withdrawing from the Account

Assuming you plan to live another 35 years to age 100, how much can you take out each month as supplemental retirement income? More than you might expect.

As shown in Table 7-9, from this $300,000 principal you would draw $1,771 monthly, for an annual withdrawal of $21,252. Your total withdrawal over the 35 years would be $743,820. After 35 years of withdrawals, the entire account would be depleted.

Table 7-9
Distributions From a $300,000 Principal Over 35 Years

Monthly Payments Received	$1,771
Annualized	$21,252
Total Paid Out Over 35 Years	$743,820
Balance at End of 35 Years	0

So you made monthly contributions of $211 over 35 years, and then you withdrew monthly payouts of $1,771 for 35 years.

How could this happen?

This is the magic of compounding. As you make the monthly contributions of $211 over 35 years, the interest compounds month after month, year after year, and the result is $300,000 from which you can draw. When you start your monthly withdrawals of $1,771, from the $300,000 corpus, the balance left in the account continues to earn interest.

Table 7-10
Funding a Target Amount of $500,000 Over 35 Years

Monthly Payments	$351
Annualized	$4,212
Total Paid In Over 35 Years	$147,420
Value of Account After 35 Years	$500,000

Another Example

Suppose you wanted to have a target amount of $500,000 at retirement age, Tables 7-10 and 7-11 show how that works.

As shown in Table 7-10, you would need to contribute $351 monthly, for an annual contribution of $4,212. Your total contribution over the 35 years would be $147,420. And now, at age 65, you have $500,000 to draw from.

Table 7-11
Distributions From a $500,000 Principal Over 35 Years

Monthly Payments Received	$2,851
Annualized	$34,212
Total Paid Out Over 35 Years	$1,197,420
Balance at End of 35 Years	0

As shown in Table 7-11, from this $500,000 principal, you would draw $2,851 monthly for an annual withdrawal of $34,212. Your total withdrawal over the 35 years would be $1,197,420. After 35 years of withdrawals, the entire account would be depleted.

Annuities

An annuity is a payment made to you by an insurance company. You give the company money in one lump sum. Or, you can give the money bit by bit, as monthly payments over a period of years. This is referred to as the *accumulation* or *funding phase* of an annuity. The company will invest your money, and at a predetermined date, usually age 65, will make monthly payments to you for the rest of your life. This is referred to as the *liquidation* or *distribution phase*.

Fixed and Variable Annuities

The amount of the payment may be a set amount, known as a *fixed annuity*. Or it might be different amounts in different years. This is known as a *variable annuity*. Or it could be a combination of both. The details on these accounts will differ from company to company, and will depend on such factors as your age at the payout time, your expected longevity, the prevailing interest rate at the time of the initial payment you make, and a myriad of other factors.

Are Annuities a Good Deal?

But let's back up a moment. Strictly speaking, the term *annuity* is short for an *annuity contract*. When you enter into an annuity contract with an insurance company, you agree to give them money at a given time, and they agree to distribute money to you at a later date. The money is no longer yours. It belongs to the insurance company. They have the money, and you have their promise to distribute it to you later. That's the contract.

There are benefits to having an annuity contract.

- It disciplines you to put money away for retirement.
- The money compounds on a tax-deferred basis.
- It distributes money to you at regular monthly intervals, so you can't blow the whole investment on a whim.
- It is often combined with a life insurance policy to give added protection to your wealth.

But there are drawbacks as well.

- The money is distributed to you whether you want it or not, and only in amounts agreed to by the contract.
- Your investment in the annuity is not your money; it's the company's.

- There are expenses involved in maintaining your account, for which you will be charged.
- Also, there is often a hefty sales charge, which is taken from your investment at the beginning.

Annuities are right for some people, and inappropriate for others. I don't necessarily endorse them or discourage people from buying them. Whether it's right for you or not will depend on many personal and idiosyncratic characteristics. For example, are you a saver and your spouse is a spender? And if you die, would he or she receive an inheritance and blow the whole thing at once? Having your money in an annuity would ensure steady payments over your spouse's life so the money would last.

Funding An Annuity
The examples above are based on hypothetical situations. Here's a real-life example of the effect of the early investing of a very small sum over a long period of time and letting it sit there to compound.

Time: 1973 to 1983
Amount invested: $30 per month for nine months of each of ten years; $270 per year.
Total amount invested: $2,700; no further investments made after 1983.
Investment vehicles: 50% fixed income fund, 50% common stock fund; earnings compounded tax-free
Value on June 1, 2000: $51,932

Table 7-12 Example of Funding an Annuity	
Monthly Payments	$30
Annualized (Nine-Month Year)	$270
Total Paid In Over 10 Years	$2,700
Years of Compounding After 10 Year Period	17
Account value in Year 2000	$51,932

This example in Table 7-12 shows that even very small amounts can compound into sizable chunks of cash, given enough years.

Cashing In on an Annuity

The investor in this example decided to begin drawing on this amount at age 65, and rather than take the money in a lump sum, decided to annuitize[7] it, thus receiving monthly payments of about $300, as shown in Table 7-13.

Table 7-13	
Monthly Annuities From $51,932 Principal Over Expected Longevity	
Monthly Payments Received	$280-305
Annualized	$3,360-3,660

Beautiful! He invested that $270 per <u>year</u> for ten years, and now receives even more, $300 per <u>month</u> for the rest of his life.

Annuitize Your Investments

You can take the concept of an annuity contract with an insurance company, and apply it yourself, rather than with an insurance company. If you have the discipline to do this, it can be a lot cheaper and equally as effective as most annuity contracts with insurance companies. Here's the way it might work.

Go back to Table 7-10. As shown, you contribute $351 monthly for 35 years to an account yielding 6% compounded monthly, you would have an account balance of $500,000. Table 7-11 shows how you can make monthly withdrawals of $2,851 for 35 years to deplete the account.

This is a "do-it-yourself" annuity. It saves a considerable amount of money in sales and administrative costs to do it this way,

---

7   An annuity is a monthly payment based on an amount of principal, which payment can be made for the duration of a person's life. The annuity in this example was in a supplemental retirement account, and was invested with an insurance company.

in contrast to an annuity contract with an insurance company. However, there are two facts of which you must be aware.

- Unless this account is in a 403(b) account or other tax-advantaged account, such as an annuity offered by an insurance company, you will be required to pay taxes on all earnings, whether dividends, interest, or capital gains, in the year when you receive them.
- Also, inflation over the 70 years of these contributions and withdrawals will have eroded the purchasing power of the money in question.

On the positive side, however, there are advantages to doing it yourself.

- The money invested remains yours, not the insurance company's.
- If you die prematurely, the money will be part of your estate, and can be bequeathed to your heirs.
- You can take as much, or as little, from the account at any given time, rather than receive monthly payments from the insurance annuity.

Other Funds for Retirement

The last category of retirement funding is the investments you make outside of the categories described above. These are your non-retirement investments found in your taxable accounts. The next two chapters will describe the various investments that can be made to accumulate wealth, usable at any time for any desired purpose, including providing retirement income.

CHAPTER EIGHT
INVESTING AND WEALTH CREATION

If you've come to this point of the book, you know that you should be running your household like a small business. You know how much you're worth from Chapter Two; you know how to track your cash coming in and going out, and how to budget for your expenses from Chapter Three. Further, you know how to get value for your purchases and how to avoid wasting money from Chapters Four and Five. You know how to use debt wisely from Chapter Six. And finally, you have an idea of how to plan for the financial aspects of your retirement from Chapter Seven.

This chapter picks up where we left off discussing retirement, where I presented the various sources of retirement income. After retirement funding through employment-related accounts, Social Security, and individual retirement funds, the final category is non-retirement funds. Most of this money will be the result of prudent investing during your pre-retirement years. This investing is done to create wealth to be used for retirement funding, or for any other purpose you choose.

Wealth Creation
The wealth referred to here is financial wealth, also known as money, in any of its forms. Financial wealth is sometimes called "filthy lucre" (and not necessarily in a joking manner) by those who disparage its existence, as well as its acquisition. Money is an easily misunderstood commodity. Indeed, some governments have economic policies that actively discourage the acquisition of wealth. But such thinking usually results in a low level of economic development, and a correspondingly low standard of living for everyone. Overall, this is not good for the people the government seeks to serve. It doesn't have to be this way. Witness what's been going on in China.

China and Wealth

Since the mid-twentieth century, the People's Republic of China had a communist government that implemented central planning, resulting in a controlled economy. The economy grew very slowly and poverty was rampant, with most people living as they did in the 19th century. In the 1980s, Deng Xiaoping changed the country's direction with the statement, "To get rich, is glorious," and freed his country from the shackles of central planning. This unleashed the entrepreneurial spirit of the Chinese people, and the rest is history.

Wealth is Good.
Money is Good.
Everyone Should Have Some.

Myths and Half-Truths About Money

Let's start off our presentation of wealth creation by dispelling some myths and half-truths about money.

Money is the root of all evil. Myth

Money is <u>not</u> the root of all evil. This is a misquote from Scripture, and is a myth on three counts. The actual quote from Scripture states that, "the <u>love</u> of money is <u>a</u> root of <u>all</u> <u>kinds</u> <u>of</u> evil" (emphasis added). The misquote leaves out the "love" part, and changes the article from "a" to "the", and changes "all kinds of evil" to "all evil."

Money is a commodity, and as such it is neutral. It can be used for good or bad purposes. Money should not be loved. It's not worthy of love. People, animals, flowers, ideas, music, art, and fine wine – those things are worthy of love. But not money.

Money cannot buy happiness. Half-truth

Money can give you financial security, but not necessarily happiness. Of course, it is true that money cannot buy happiness <u>directly</u>, but it might buy happiness <u>indirectly</u> by allowing freedom from drudgery work, or permitting a better standard of living. But even this doesn't work for everyone. Many people who win the lottery are at first in a state of euphoria, but a few years later, they are right back to being about as happy or unhappy as they were before their windfall. And on top of that, often the money is all gone.

There is an increasing body of research in neuroscience to indicate that a person's propensity to be happy is, in part, genetically driven. Most psychologists agree that only a small portion of people's happiness is a reflection of their financial status. Indeed, about half people's happiness can be attributed to differences in their genes. In other words, some people seem born to be happy, and others not. But free will still enters into the equation. Perhaps Abraham Lincoln said it best: "Most people are about as happy as they want to be."

If you want happiness, don't seek it directly. That's futile. Happiness comes from inside you and is a result of what you are and what you do, not what you have. My favorite quotation on the subject expresses it beautifully: "Happiness is like a butterfly. The more you chase it, the more it eludes you. But if you go peacefully about your business, it comes to sit quietly on your shoulder."

So be happy. But also remember the words of famed investor Warren Buffett, "Happiness does not buy money."

Investing in stocks is like gambling. Half-truth
For people who know something about basic economics and what stock ownership represents, and who invest knowingly, with specific purposes in mind, investing is not gambling. But this is not so for all people. Some people view investing as one big crapshoot, another kind of game similar to blackjack, roulette, and others found in the casinos of Las Vegas. They are gamblers. I recall in 1998, at the height of the dot-com madness, seeing a posting on a company message board by a newcomer stating, "Hi, everybody. I just bought 100 shares of this company. What do they do?"

Everyone knows of a person who got a hot tip from his brother-in-law about a stock that was going to quadruple in three weeks, bought a few hundred or a few thousand shares, and then watched in agony as the price dived, never to recover. That's gambling, just like the lady who wanted to know what business the company was in after she had bought the stock. People who are serious about wealth accumulation through ownership of financial assets do extensive research on what they are buying, carefully measuring risk with potential reward. Or they hire people to do such research. That's investing, and it's a lot different from gambling.

I know of people who will spend hours poring over issues of *Consumer Reports* before they buy a $150 DVD player, but who will put several thousand dollars into a stock they know nothing about. I recommend that people who want to gamble go to the gaming tables at Las Vegas. Have some good food and drink, see a few shows, lose some money at the tables, and come home having had a good time. Just keep gambling separate from investing.

Young people should invest in stocks, older people, in bonds. Half-truth
Whether to invest in stocks or bonds depends on many factors other than age, such as risk tolerance, time horizon, and income needs, as we shall see in later chapters. Yes, some older people need the steady income provided by bonds, but others have generous pensions, which when added to their Social Security, give them more than enough current income. If they were not invested at least partially in common stocks, they could be missing opportunities for great accumulation of wealth.

You need to be lucky to be rich. Half-truth
Some people are lucky to have chosen wealthy parents. Others are lucky because they won the state lottery. Luck is good, to be sure. And you are better off with it than without it. But intelligent

decisions about investing can go a long way toward changing bad luck or no luck into good luck.

In investing, we apply our knowledge and intelligence to our research efforts. This is called *due diligence*, and it's amazing how this effort can change a person's luck. Just keep in mind the quotations of these two leading sports figures: Golfer Gary Player said, "The more I practice, the luckier I get." And the legendary football coach Vince Lombardi stated, "Luck is what happens when training meets opportunity." You can make your own luck just the way you can make your own happiness.

You have to have money to make money. Half-truth

Of course, if you start with a lot of money and invest it wisely, you will probably make more money than someone who starts with nothing. But even persons of relatively modest means, who have the discipline to spend less than they earn, and who invest prudently over an extended period of time, can accumulate significant wealth. There is no secret to this. It's called living within your means, and having a plan to accumulate wealth.

In order to know the appropriate action to take in order to create wealth, there are some fundamental concepts of which you need to be aware. Understanding these concepts helps you make more informed investing decisions, and increases your likelihood of success.

Saving vs. Investing

Saving money is a good place to start your journey toward financial independence. Money saved can be stored in a coffee can buried in your backyard, or perhaps under a mattress. Assuming no one finds out about this cache of cash, your money will be safe. However, if history is any guide, as time goes on, the money will have less purchasing power due to the negative effects of inflation. So the coffee can idea has limited merit. Besides, it's inconvenient to go digging in the dirt behind your house.

Saving in Banks

Banks[1] can be helpful here. They will accept deposits of your money and put it in an account that you can access as needed. If it's a checking account, you'll have immediate access to it, and they may pay you a little interest. If it's a savings account, there may be some restrictions on the money's accessibility, but you'll be paid more interest than a checking account. Another possible account is a money market account, on which interest is paid, but generally there is a limit on the number or minimum amounts of checks written on the account. You may also purchase a Certificate of Deposit (CD) at a bank. There may be further restrictions regarding accessibility, but you'll be paid more interest than the other accounts just mentioned. Most banks are members of the Federal Deposit Insurance Corporation (FDIC), and your money will be insured up to a maximum of $100,000. If the bank fails, the FDIC will make you whole.[2]

No Risk of Principal

These bank accounts are some ways to begin saving money. Since the accounts are insured, there is no risk involved. However, interest rates will differ among the various accounts for savings. Your checking account will probably pay you the lowest interest rate, so keep enough money in it to pay for your regular monthly expenses with a small margin for safety. Next is your savings account, which pays more interest than the checking account. Keep money in this account for emergencies, or for anticipated expenditures that will occur within the year. For expected expenditure in time periods longer than one year, save the money in one or more certificates of deposit (CDs). They pay the highest interest.

If you are fortunate, the interest you will receive in the savings and CD accounts will exceed the rate of inflation, although this is rarely the case. If it is, then you will have little or no risk of los-

---

1   The term *banks*, as used here, includes credit unions.
2   The National Credit Union Administration (NCUA), a government agency, insures accounts in credit unions. Coverage is similar to that provided by the FDIC.

ing purchasing power to inflation. This brings us to the next fundamental concept, risk and reward.

Risk and Reward

Risk is the chance you take that you will lose some or all of your money. *Reward* is the benefit you get from saving or investing, and usually comes in the form of money received as dividends, interest, or in the profits (realized or unrealized) from the increase in an asset's value.

The bank accounts just described bear no risk, but they don't offer much reward either. The fundamental concept is that as risk increases, so does potential reward. And conversely, as reward increases, so does potential risk. This is an immutable law. There are no exceptions. You don't get something for nothing in financial matters, and if someone ever promises you a "guaranteed" high financial reward for little or no risk, run – don't walk – away. It just ain't gonna happen.

Stocks vs. Bonds

Stocks,[3] also known as *equity*, represent ownership interests in corporations. When a corporation makes money, its owners, the stockholders, often benefit from a rising stock price and/or an initial or increased dividend. When a corporation loses money, its owners, the stockholders, often suffer from a declining stock price and/or decreased dividend.

More Risk in Stocks

There is no guarantee that a corporation will make money. It depends on overall business conditions, the quality of management, and a myriad of other factors. Stocks do not mature – in other words, they are not redeemed after a certain period. They live on as long as the corporation is an ongoing business entity.

---

3   The stocks referred to here are common stocks. There are also financial instruments known as preferred stocks, bond-like instruments, which are not appropriate for most readers of this book. Preferred stocks are usually purchased by financial institutions and other corporations, and not individuals.

Less Risk in Bonds

On the other hand, bonds, also known as *debt*, do not represent ownership interests. Rather, they represent obligations of the corporations to pay interest to bondholders in a timely manner, and, at their maturity, return to them the principal invested. In other words, bonds are IOUs that have a limited life.

Price Variation between Stock and Bonds

Stock prices of a corporation vary, sometimes considerably, over a period of time. Bond prices vary too, but not nearly as much as stock prices. That's because bondholders expect to get their investment back at a certain time, the maturity date. Stockholders may never get their investment back. For this reason, investments in bonds are considered generally safer than stocks.

Research on investment markets over a period of many decades shows that taken collectively, investments in common stocks yield higher returns over time than bonds. The important phrase here is "over time." In periods of recession such as the 1930s or the 1970s, stocks went nowhere while bonds returned a steady income. On the other hand, in the expansionary environment of the 1960s and the 1990s, common stocks did much better than bonds. Then, in the first few years of the 21st century, bonds did better than stocks. Economic conditions change, and markets change. You are going to be a long-term investor, so the ups and downs of the stock market will not affect you in the long run.

That brings us to the concept of time horizon.

Time Horizon

Will you need this money next week, next year, in five years, in ten years, in 20 years? The period during which your money will not need to be accessed is your *time horizon*. If you have a short time horizon, savings are appropriate. And if your time horizon is longer, then investments may be more appropriate.

When Do You Need the Money?

During the strong bull market in the 1990s, I heard a radio interview with a man who had followed his broker's advice, and had invested money from his child's college fund in a small company's stock. The investment went sour, and he lost all the money. He angrily berated his broker saying, "Hey. What'd you do? My kid's going to college next year. That money was for his college expenses." I suspect he didn't know what he was doing by making this type of investment. But certainly his broker should have known.

The first problem was his time horizon. Money that will be needed in a short time should not be invested in stocks. Individual stocks, and the stock market in general, have risks. If you need to have money in a short time, an individual stock and/or the overall stock market at that time may be lower than when you invested. Money needed within the next few years should be in savings, not investments.

And, of course, the second problem was that the company was a poor investment.

Risk Tolerance

As noted earlier, risk and reward go hand in hand. The greater the risk, the greater the potential reward. The less the risk, the less the potential reward. How much risk a person should take is a key decision in an effort to accumulate wealth. Let's start with a basic fact: All investments have some degree of risk, and stocks are riskier than bonds.

All Investments Have Some Risk

Over time, stocks have a higher total return than bonds, even though they fluctuate considerably more. As seen by the booming economy of the 1990s, the recession as the century turned, and the economic recovery that took place in 2003, it is clear that the business cycle has not been repealed. Sometimes stocks are a better investment than bonds, and sometimes bonds are a better investment than stocks. And sometimes cash equivalents are the best investment. And what action the Federal Reserve Board takes has an overarching effect on everything.

Thus, in determining how much risk is appropriate for a given investor, consideration must be given to time horizons, risk tolerance, and macroeconomic conditions, as well as many other factors, as will be presented later. But the basic fact remains: Risk and reward go hand in hand. I believe that moderate, controlled risk is the best way to approach long-term investing for wealth accumulation.

Risk and Time Horizon
How much risk should a person take in making investments for wealth accumulation? There are several factors to be considered while answering this question. A person's time horizon is of the utmost importance. If a 35-year-old is investing for retirement at age 65, an investment in a diversified portfolio of common stocks may be the best investment. On the other hand, if this same person needs to have cash available in a few years to pay for college tuition for one or more children, placing the money in one of the savings accounts described previously probably would be better.

Moderate risk is good
Before you save, or invest in any financial instrument, you need to ask yourself how much risk you can tolerate. That question will depend on what you are going to do with the money saved or invested, and how long it will be until you need to access the money (i.e., your time horizon).

Investors vary widely in their risk tolerance. At one end of the spectrum is a non-investment: stuffing the cash into the mattress. Aside from the obvious risk of loss from theft or fire, there is a significant inflation risk.[4] In other words, when the money is

---

4   In the last 25 years, inflation has varied from 2% to 5%, with an average rate of a bit less than 3%.

taken from the mattress to be spent, its purchasing power may very well have diminished.

Very Risky Stuff
At the other end of the investment spectrum is the investment in penny stocks or IPOs (initial public offerings) of start-up corporations with no history, no earnings, perhaps no revenues, and a very uncertain future. The professionals who do this are the *venture capitalists*, or *angel investors*. They have the knowledge and skills with which to analyze the potential profitability of a new company, and they invest with their eyes open. Sometimes they hit grand slam home runs, but more often than not, they strike out.

When individual investors, just plain people like you and me, engage in this kind of investing, we are getting close to the line that separates investing from gambling. There are some people who invest their assets in this manner, who have a lot of discretionary cash that they can afford to lose, so they roll the dice and take their chances. I'm not one of those people, and I expect that neither are you.

Prudent Investing
Between the mattress stuffers and the gamblers are the prudent investors, who put their money in established stocks, bonds, real estate, commodities, etc. I believe that money should be invested, not hidden away or gambled. This means that investors will have to accept some risk that their investment may not turn out the way they anticipated.

The fact is that markets fluctuate. The fact is that money can be lost, as well as gained, as a result of investing it. Another fact is that no one can predict the future, but looking at the past can give us some guidance as to what the future might hold. I write guidance, not certainty.

A major consideration in prudent investing is to know, for any investment you make, what the risks are, and balance them with the potential rewards. You need to know both. It is amazing to me how often this principle is violated – even by those who are professionals in the field of finance.

They Should Have Known Better

In 1994, the Orange County, California investment fund filed for bankruptcy. This was the fund that invested the county's money to finance its pensions, among other obligations. Apparently, the fund manager had used derivatives, financial instruments that can provide enormous leverage but are very interest-rate sensitive, to increase the fund's returns. He bet big, and he lost big. When queried about this ill-fated strategy, he admitted that he really didn't understand the risks involved in using derivatives.

More recently, in 2008, holders of auction-rate securities, touted as being as safe and as liquid as money market funds, were surprised to find out that there was no market for their securities. So much for liquidity! They were stuck with the securities, and the banks, which had advised their customers to purchase these instruments, were under pressure from the New York Attorney General's office to return the investors' money. Auction-rate securities have their rates set at periodic auctions. I wonder if anyone ever asked, "What happens if no one shows up for the auction?" Because that's exactly what happened.

Liquidity

This refers to the ease with which you can convert your investment into cash, either greenbacks or a checking account. Vehicles like checking accounts are very *liquid* – indeed, they may define liquidity. On the other hand, real estate or thinly-traded bonds are considered illiquid. They cannot be readily converted to cash.

The most liquid vehicles where money can be placed – checking accounts, savings accounts, money market accounts, and short term CDs – have virtually no risk (but also comparatively low rewards). They are appropriate for persons who:
- are extremely averse to risk (<u>very</u> low risk tolerance)
- have a short time horizon
- need instant liquidity

Funding Your RD/CE Fund

The money for your Rainy Day/Capital Expense Fund, as described in earlier chapters, should be placed in savings vehicles such as those described above. Remember, the purpose of the RD/CE is to have readily available funds for an emergency, such as losing your job, or for making a capital expense, such as a new car.

Suppose you lose your job. You'll need money to tide you over until you get another job, or somehow replace that income. Money for this purpose should be in a savings or money market account, since you have a short time horizon and liquidity is essential.

On the other hand, suppose you already have money put away for a situation like a lost job, where there is an imminent need for liquidity. However, you plan to buy a car in about a year. Money for that purpose can be put in a CD that has a twelve-month maturity. This financial instrument will give you a better return than the checking or savings account.

Guidelines for Successful Investing

Here are five principles to guide your investing:

- Invest prudently. Don't gamble.
- Invest in financial instruments you understand.
- Invest on a regular basis, perhaps using dollar cost averaging as described in the next chapter.
- Invest for the long term. Don't let short-term market volatility divert your focus.
- And finally, be patient. Wealth accumulation takes time.

This chapter has presented information that is vital to understanding how to build wealth. The next chapter will continue this pattern, and deal with some specifics on how to invest.

CHAPTER NINE
ACCUMULATING WEALTH

In the last chapter, I presented some fundamental information about wealth, money, and investing. This chapter continues by applying this information to wealth accumulation.

Investing

When saving money, your funds are in insured accounts. There is no risk. However, as noted earlier, the rewards from these savings are very low. When you <u>invest</u>, you take on more risk, but you do so with the expectation that the potential rewards from your investment will make the risk worthwhile. Investing should be done with funds that will not be needed for <u>at least</u> five or six years. In other words, you need a long time horizon, and no immediate need for liquidity for investing. However, as you get closer to the time when you may need to withdraw funds from the investments, you'll need to shift some of the funds to a more liquid account.

With investing, a basic rule is that the potential reward from an investment must be commensurate with the riskiness of the investment. If you want a large return on your investment, you will have to take some large risks. If you will settle for a moderate return on your investment, the risks you take will be accordingly moderate. This moderate approach is called *conservative investing,* and it's what I recommend.

When to Begin

I recommend a very linear approach to investing. Before you invest in non-retirement accounts, there are some necessary preconditions.

1. **Your Net Worth Statement should be positive.** If it is negative, you have to pay off "bad" debt to make it positive. (See Chapter Two)

2. **Your Cash Flow Statement should be positive.** If you are running at a deficit, that has to be fixed, either by earning more or spending less. (See Chapters Three, Four, and Five.)
3. **You should have little or no "bad" debt (credit cards, store cards, etc.).** And you should pay it off at the end of every month so as not to incur interest charges. (See Chapter Six)
4. **You should have started funding your Rainy Day/Capital Expense fund.** This is the key to financial success. (Again, see Chapter Six)
5. **You should have funded your retirement accounts as much as you can.** These are tax-favored accounts that allow rapid compounding. Also, your employer might be making a contribution, and you wouldn't want to miss out on that. (See Chapter Seven)

If you meet these five criteria, you're ready to invest in non-retirement accounts.

Investing should be done carefully and prudently. There are some basic principles you need to consider. But first, you may ask, "Do I really have to know this stuff? Can't I just turn over my money to someone else and have him or her invest it for me?" The answer to the first question is <u>yes</u>. And the answer to the second question is <u>no</u>.

Why You Need To Know This Stuff

If you are like most young people, you know very little, or perhaps nothing, about investing. That's all right. But you are a consumer of financial services. And like any other consumer buying any other product, you need to know what the product is, how it works, and what the risks are in using it. You probably do this when you buy a car, or a refrigerator, or even a can of soup. Well, you need to know this about financial products, which are, for the most part, intangible instruments representing real assets, and which can generate real money. For newcomers to personal finance, it may seem foreign and confusing. But so was long division, which you learned in fourth grade.

There Are Some Bad Guys Out There

A second, but equally important, factor is that you must be careful to avoid being taken advantage of. There are some people who delegate the responsibility of managing their wealth to professionals in the field. Unfortunately, not all of these professionals are honest, and they can wreak havoc upon your chances for financial success. These rascals come in all sizes, shapes, nationalities, races, religions, ethnicities, and both genders.

Affinity Scams

Some of the most flagrant violations of trust are often done by people you think you know and can trust. Or by someone endorsed by your minister, priest, or rabbi. This can lead to *affinity scams*. Is this kind of operation, typically a member of your church, synagogue, ethnic group, or neighborhood, whom you have no reason to distrust, takes advantage of you by engaging in a *Ponzi scheme*. He or she takes investors' money, promising a high return on the money received, but may not be forthcoming with information about the investments supposedly being made. He or she might say, "It's okay. Don't worry. It's probably too difficult for you to understand. Trust me. It'll be fine."

Then the schemer finds some new investors, and uses their money to pay a cash return to the original investors. Then the process repeats with yet another set of investors, and so on. While investors are being bilked out of their money, the schemer may be living "the good life," with expensive houses and cars, exotic vacations, etc. Or perhaps the money will be gambled away. Or perhaps it will find itself in a numbered bank account somewhere. But one place it will probably not be found is in legitimate investments.

> ### From the Headlines
> In 2008, investment manager Bernard Madoff allegedly combined an affinity scam with a Ponzi scheme. He lost more than $5 billion of his clients' money.

Be Careful Out There

Sooner or later, these schemers are found out, brought to justice, and punished. But rarely are the investors made whole. The moral of the story is that when there is a lot of money to be made, predators will come forward to help separate you from your money. Most people are kind and decent folks, but there are some bad players out there. Be careful.

With this understanding, let's get started investing by understanding the timeless, basic principle of diversification.

Diversification

A key concept in investing is to *diversify* your assets. You've probably heard the old saying, "Don't keep all your eggs in one basket." As applied to investing, this means don't put all your money in only one single stock or only one asset classification (stocks, bonds, commodities).

Investing in Mutual Funds: Instant Diversification

Mutual funds and their new-on-the-scene cousins, Exchange Traded Funds (EFTs), provide a means for beginning investors, with limited resources, to invest in a diversified stock portfolio. In a mutual fund, your investment is pooled with that of other investors in purchasing a basketful of stocks. Exactly which stocks are in the basket will depend upon the mission of a particular fund, as we shall see shortly.

Dollar Cost Averaging

Dollar cost averaging is an effective way to build wealth through systematic, periodic investments of relatively small amounts of money over a given period of time. It is a perfect way of investing in mutual funds.

Market risk is the risk that the share price will at times be lower after you make the stock investment. Dollar cost averaging reduces market risk by averaging down the cost of your shares purchased over a period of time.

Dollar Cost Averaging and Market Risk

Here's the way it works. Say you make a monthly investment of $100 in a mutual fund that you expect to redeem when you retire. The share price of the fund varies from month to month. In the first month, the fund might be selling at $25 per share. Your $100 would buy 4 shares. The next month, the share price might be $23, and you would have bought 4.35 shares. The following month, the share price might be $27, and your $100 would have bought 3.70 shares. By purchasing the same dollar amount each month, when the share price is higher you buy fewer shares, and when the share price is lower you buy more shares.

When It's Low, Buy More

Table 9-1 shows how dollar cost averaging works with a monthly investment of $100, in a mutual fund that varies in price from $23 to $29 per share over a twelve-month period.

After 12 monthly investments of $100 each, a total of $1,200 invested, the total number of shares owned is 47.03. At the cur-

Table 9-1 Example of Dollar Cost Averaging			
Amount Invested	Share Price	Shares Purchased	Cumulative Shares Owned
$100	$25	4.00	4.00
$100	$27	3.70	7.70
$100	$28	3.57	11.27
$100	$24	4.17	15.44
$100	$23	4.35	19.79
$100	$23	4.35	24.14
$100	$24	4.17	28.31
$100	$25	4.00	32.31
$100	$26	3.85	36.16
$100	$28	3.85	40.01
$100	$28	3.57	43.58
$100	$29	3.45	47.03

rent price of $29 per share, this investment is worth $1,364 (47.03 shares times $29). The average cost of each share is $25.52.

Constant Share Purchasing

With Constant Share Purchasing, instead of investing the same <u>dollar amount</u> monthly, the investor decides to buy <u>a constant number of shares</u> every month over the same 12 months. Table 9-2 shows how constant share purchasing works with a monthly investment of $100, in a mutual fund that varies in price from $23 to $29 per share over a twelve-month period. (These are the same prices and the same period as in the dollar cost averaging example in Table 9-1.)

Table 9-2
Example of Constant Share Purchasing

Number of Shares Purchased	Share Price	Cost	Cumulative Shares Owned
4	$25	$100	4
4	$27	$108	8
4	$28	$112	12
4	$24	$96	16
4	$23	$92	20
4	$23	$92	24
4	$24	$96	28
4	$25	$100	32
4	$26	$104	36
4	$28	$112	40
4	$28	$112	44
4	$29	$116	48

After 12 monthly purchases of four shares per month, a total of 48 shares were purchased, representing a total investment of $1,240. At the current price of $29, the investment is worth $1,392 (48 shares times $29). The average cost of each share is $25.83.

Comparing the Two Strategies

Table 9-3 contrasts the two approaches to investing, constant dollar amount (a.k.a. dollar cost averaging) and constant share amount.

Table 9-3 — Comparison of Constant Dollar and Constant Share Amount Investing					
Investing Strategy	Amount invested	Number of Shares Purchased	Average Cost	Value at $29 per Share	Rate of Return on Investment
Dollar Cost	$1,200	47.03	$25.67	$1,364	13.67%
Constant Share	$1,240	48.00	$25.83	$1,392	12.26%

Table 9-3 shows the average cost of a share with dollar cost method is $25.67, only sixteen cents less than the constant share method's $25.83. This is not a large amount of money, to be sure. But look at the last column showing the rate of return on each investment. The return on the dollar cost investment is 13.67%. The return on the constant share investment is 12.26%, a difference of 1.41%.

Time and the Rate of Return

The examples given in the tables above show results in a twelve-month period. In actuality, though, long-term investing entails time frames of decades. And over time, and with continuous compounding, the difference between a return of 12.26% and 13.67% can represent a sizable amount of money.

Take a look at Table 9-4. This shows the value of monthly investments of $100, compounded monthly over 20 years, at the two rates of return (interest rates) shown in Table 9-3.

Table 9-4 — Compounding of $100 per Month at Two Interest Rates	
Interest Rate	Value in 20 Years
13.67%	$124,280
12.26%	$102,400
Difference	$21,880

At the compounding rate of 13.67%, the value of the investments would have been $124,280. At the compounding rate of 12.26%, the value of the investments would have been $102,400, a difference of $21,880. Thus, a small difference in the investment yield can make a large difference in the final result.

Types of Mutual Funds

At last count, there are more than 8,000 mutual funds, more than the number of stocks on the New York Stock Exchange. The equity and debt markets are sliced and diced in many different ways, too numerous to mention except for a few examples.

Stock Funds – Here are some representative mutual funds in the equity market.

- Index funds: collections of stocks that represent a broad, identifiable group of companies, such as the Standard & Poor's 500 (the S&P 500), the Dow Jones Industrials (the Dow), and others
- Sector Funds: an assortment of stocks in one particular sector, like health care or utilities
- Growth Funds: stocks that are expected to grow faster than other stocks
- Income Funds: stocks that provide better income through dividend payments than other stock funds
- Balanced Funds: both stocks and bonds (that's the "balance"). This type of fund provides more price stability than funds exclusively containing stocks
- International Funds: stocks in corporations that are headquartered outside the United States

- Target Retirement Funds: a blend of stocks and bonds that will vary over the time prior to a target year. The buyer selects a target year, perhaps the anticipated year for retirement, and the fund automatically changes the proportions of stocks and bonds to decrease the stock proportion and increase the bond proportion as the target date approaches. These funds are relatively new financial products, and may be considered as a special type of balanced fund, with the rebalancing taking place every year.

Bond Funds – Here are some representative mutual funds in the debt market. Also, for most bond funds, there are taxable and non-taxable versions.

- Treasury Bonds: U.S. Treasury bonds.
- Short-Term Bonds: bonds with nearer maturity
- Long-Term Bonds: bonds with later maturity
- Junk Bonds: bonds of questionable safety that pay high interest
- Municipal Bonds: bonds of states and municipalities

Your Investment Strategy
Let's look at you and your situation.

- You are young. You have a long time horizon, so investments in stocks should be a prominent portion of your investments.
- You are a prudent investor, not a gambler, and not an overly fearful person, so you can accept a moderate level of risk.
- You don't have a lot of money to start with, and you need to diversify your investments.

In light of these characteristics, investing in mutual funds is probably your best move. Now the question is, which ones?

There are several configurations:
- Invest in several mutual funds: 75% in a stock index fund, 15% a bond fund, and 10% in an international fund.
- Invest in one balanced fund and one international fund.
- Invest 90% in a Target Year Fund with the target year being the year in which you'll need the money (the year your kid goes to college, assuming it is 15 years away, the year you plan to retire, etc.), and 10% in an international fund.

Selecting Mutual Funds

When purchasing anything, such as a car, a house, or a computer, you should seek value. This means that you want a quality product, you want to purchase it at a reasonable price, and you don't want to spend a lot of money on its maintenance. The same goes for investing in mutual funds. Let's deal with these attributes one at a time.

Quality – A quality mutual fund is one that fulfills its mission. If it's a growth mutual fund, it should perform as well or better than the average fund of the same type.

Reasonable Price – This can be had by engaging in dollar cost averaging, as explained below.

Maintenance – This is extremely important. You need to know how much this fund will cost to run itself year after year. This information can be found in the expense ratio of the fund, that is, for each $100 invested, how much money goes for administrative costs, brokerage fees, advertising expenses, etc. The higher the expense ratio, the less of your money is invested productively. If you want to accumulate wealth, you want to pay the minimum in fund expenses.

Watch Your Expenses

In some respects, accumulating wealth is like trying to have a profit in a business. The formula is a simple one:

For a business
Revenues – Expenses = Profits

For wealth accumulation
Investment Income – Expenses = Additional Wealth

By applying this formula in business, you can increase your accumulated wealth either by increasing income, reducing expenses, or both. No business will be successful if it doesn't carefully monitor its expenses. You, as an investor in mutual funds, need to do the same thing.

Here are some ideas on how to reduce your investment expenses.

1. When you invest in mutual funds, find the funds that do not have a sales load (front or back), a marketing expense, or any other unnecessary charges.
2. Any financial product that is presented to you through a salesperson is going to cost more than the same product purchased without the salesperson. Salespersons are paid for their services, as they should be, and the salary or commission they receive is an expense that is really paid by you, since it is included in the price you pay for the product. Ask yourself if you need to be sold this product, or in contrast, if you can purchase it independent of the salesperson.
3. Use tax-efficient, tax-reduced, or tax-avoided investment vehicles as much as possible.
4. Invest in mutual funds that have low annual expenses. This figure is expressed as a dollar amount per $100 invested. The lower, the better. A stock index fund should have an expense ratio of less than 0.25%. This means

that of every \$100 invested, only ¼ of 1%, 25 cents, is spent on running the fund. \$99.75 is invested on your behalf. An international fund's expense ratio might be expected to be somewhat higher, in the neighborhood of 1%-1.5%.

5. Some investments are virtual commodities, like index funds or money market funds. As with other commodities that you buy in your everyday life (gasoline, flour, sugar), there are often barely noticeable differences between them. So buy the cheapest ones you can, the ones with the lowest expenses. If you are paying more for your commodity than someone else, be sure that you are getting value for the premium you are paying.

6. Use dollar cost averaging to your benefit. Month after month, in good times and in bad times, keep investing the same dollar amount. After a number of years, you'll be glad you did.

Investing for the Long-Term

Earlier in this chapter, I recommended a very linear approach to investing.

1. Your Net Worth Statement should be positive.
2. Your Cash Flow Statement should be positive.
3. You should have little or no bad debt (credit cards, store cards, etc).
4. You should have started funding your Rainy Day/Capital Expense fund.
5. You should have funded your retirement accounts as much as you can.

Let's pick up on point #5.

Funding Your Retirement Funds

As discussed in Chapter Seven, retirement accounts are an excellent vehicle for long-term investing, and should be funded as much as possible. Their tax-deferred compounding properties, along with their before-tax features, make them superior to many other types of accounts. Now, what to put in them?

If you are in your 20s or 30s, and your employer's plan gives you a choice, your money should be allotted as follows: 65% stock index funds, 20% international funds, 15% bond funds. As indicated earlier, choose funds with no sales charges, low administrative and advertising charges, and low expenses per $100 of investment.

The same assortment of funds should be in your non-retirement funds, the earnings of which are, of course, taxable. But here, with taxable accounts, because you are doing the investing independent of your employment, you may have additional choices of investments. There are blended funds that might suit you, or perhaps target date funds are more to your liking.

Why Not Buy Stocks or Bonds?
As discussed earlier in this chapter, diversification is a key element of prudent investing. Mutual funds of stocks, bonds, or both, provide a ready means for instant diversification. If, as an alternative, you were to buy individual stocks such as IBM, Staples, or GE, or individual corporate bonds, you would need to have about 20 securities in each asset category to have adequate diversification in your portfolio. And to have a meaningful position in them, you'd need to invest about $100,000. At this time in your life, you probably don't have that much money for investing, so it's better to go with the mutual funds.

Buy and Hold
This approach to investing is referred to as a "buy and hold" approach. In contrast, there are "trading" approaches whereby investors zip in and out of funds based on whims. That's not for prudent, long-term investors.

If you are new at investing, and don't have the time or the inclination to follow the markets and trends, the best approach is to invest in low cost, high quality, index mutual funds, or in funds with outstanding performance records. Each year, *Forbes* magazine has several issues on mutual funds. They rate only funds that have been operational for four complete market cycles, beginning on June 30, 1994. So these funds have established track records from which their quality can be assessed.

The funds are given grades of A+ to F for their performance in both up and down market cycles. Additional information is given regarding their costs of ownership, tax efficiency, and minimum initial investment. Forbes also has a classification of mutual funds as "Best Buys," which combine low cost and good risk-adjusted performance over the last five years. Forbes is an excellent source for this important and unbiased information.

Don't try to time the investment markets

"The market's too high. I can't make any money by investing now." This complaint has been heard time and time again from would-be investors over the decades. Whenever there has been a strong bull market, people who were not invested feel left out, and don't want to get in because they think the market is too high. Of course, markets do indeed get overvalued. This happens on a regular basis. Then again, markets regularly get undervalued as well. Markets are driven by greed and fear. When greed is operative, stock prices get overvalued. When fear is operative, markets get undervalued. Markets fluctuate. Always have, and always will.

Everyone dreams of investing at the very bottom of the market, and selling at its very top. This is called market timing, and there really are people who claim they can do this. Of course they can. Anyone can. But no one has yet to be found who can do it on a <u>regular and consistent basis</u>. Even a broken clock is right twice a day.

I believe that market timing is a poor strategy. It just can't be done consistently. Bernard Baruch, the fabled investor from the early 20th century, made a huge fortune investing in common stocks, and said that he never bought a stock at its bottom or sold it at its top. So what are we lesser financial wizards to do? I recommend that investments be made over a period of months and years, over bull markets and bear markets, and let dollar cost averaging work for you. And if your time horizon is too short to allow for this (you'll need at least 5 or 6 years), you shouldn't be investing in stocks in the first place.

Forget about market timing in order to buy mutual funds at their very lowest point. Use the dollar cost averaging described above.

Investing and Insurance

In my view, the word "insurance" should often be followed by the word "protection." For most people, the best use of insurance is to protect their assets: house, car, earnings potential, investments, etc. This material is presented in Chapter Ten. However, for some, the unique features of insurance – especially the desirable taxation aspects of its earnings and its pay-out distributions – make it a worthwhile purchase.

Also, life insurance benefits can be structured to be tax-free to the beneficiary. This can provide ready cash to the recipient who would not have to wait for the settlement of an estate. Moreover, irrevocable life insurance trusts can be excellent vehicles for the preservation and distribution of wealth as part of an estate plan. There is a place for life insurance in a person's financial life, as will be presented in the next chapter. But insuring and investing are two different activities.

Keep Insurance and Investing Separate

When insurance and investing are combined, the result is usually a life insurance policy that has cash value. However, cash value life insurance policies have limited worth in a cost-effective investing plan. The life insurance aspect of the policy can be appropriate for the protection of the insured person's dependents, but the investment properties of such policies are not necessarily the best means for accumulating wealth. For most people, it's best to keep protection separate from investments.

Your Course and Your Bearings

To accumulate wealth, you need an objective, and a plan to reach that objective. The plan should consider your wealth, income, desired future wealth and income, lifestyle, family responsibilities, anticipated longevity, risk tolerance, and a myriad of other relevant factors. The plan should be followed as much as possible. If a certain type of investment is selected, then keep investing in it. For example, don't chase last year's yield in a new mutual fund by changing funds solely to capture that yield. One market sector or investment philosophy may do better than another in a given year, only to have the situation change in the next year. You need to stay the course.

Times Do Change

Times change, markets change, and what might have been an appropriate investment at one time may not be meeting your needs at another time. So you need to check your bearings. Take, for example, utility stocks. Utility stocks were highly appropriate holdings 30 or 40 years ago. Many financial advisors would have considered them the bedrock of any stock portfolio, because they provided steady dividend income with moderate growth and safety, in the context of a controlled/regulated monopoly. Indeed, this kind of security was often referred to as the kind suitable for widows and orphans, such was their safety. But in today's financial environment, they are not appropriate for all investors. The utility industry has become deregulated, and its stocks have lost their safety of principal feature. Moreover, the once steadily increasing dividends have slowed their growth, and are still subject to taxation, albeit presently at a lower rate resulting from recent changes in the tax code.

Technology Is an Example

As another example, investments in technology, telecommunications, or the Internet should be a part of any portfolio expected to grow over the years. Many of the companies in this sector didn't exist 20 or 30 years ago. Indeed, some of them have not been sold publicly until ten years ago. In the late 1990s, there were many excesses in the trading of stocks in this industry, and prices got out of hand, leading to the collapse of the market, the so-called dot-com bubble. But the industry and its component stocks remain viable long-term investments with decent potential, and will be an integral part of the economy.

So stay the course, but do check your bearings periodically.

CHAPTER TEN
PROTECT YOURSELF

Most readers of this book probably have limited wealth. Some will have more than others, but nevertheless it will probably be a small amount. If this book's ideas on achieving financial success are followed, some wealth will ensue.

Your wealth, tangible and intangible, needs to be protected. This chapter will explore the various events that can threaten your wealth, and make recommendations for protecting it. This activity is called *estate planning*, and even if you are young and don't have much of an estate, you need to pay attention to it.

Why Insurance?

Insurance, conceptually, is the transfer of risk from one party to another. For example, if you own a car, the value of that car could be diminished in a nanosecond if an accident were to occur, totaling your car. Without insurance, you're out the value of the car. That's the risk you took when you bought the car and drove it around. When you buy insurance, however, you transferred that risk to the insurance company. You paid them a premium to accept this transfer of risk, and they are left to foot the bill for your vehicular mishap. This concept of transfer of risk applies to all insurance of any type.

For many employees, especially those employed by large firms, life and health insurance coverage is part of a package of fringe benefits. Employers purchase group policies that are relatively inexpensive and have decent coverage. If you work for such an employer, that's wonderful. But if you don't, insurance coverage is something you need to take care of on your own.

Insurance is a way of protecting yourself from financial calamity.

Your insurance needs will vary according to your age, family situation, debt, and the amount of your wealth.

The insurance industry is large, profitable, and very competitive. Finding a quality company with reasonable rates is made easy through the Web. For quotes on rates for all types of insurance, go to **www.insurance.com**, or **www.4freequotes.com**. For information about the quality of an insurance company, go to **www.ambest.com**.

Life Insurance

Most readers of this book will need little, if any, life insurance. But you do need life insurance if you find yourself in either of these situations:

- If you were to die, you would leave behind people who had relied upon your income for their economic well-being, like your spouse or your children.
- If you were to die, you would leave large amounts of debt, such as a mortgage loan, that would need to be paid off so your family could continue to reside in your house.

What Kind of Life Insurance?

If you fit one of those conditions, the most appropriate life insurance for you at this time is *term insurance*. This is insurance in its simplest form. You pay a monthly premium, and if you die, your beneficiaries are paid the face amount of the policy. Depending on the policy, the premium may increase every year, or may be level for five or ten years, after which it will be raised for the next five or ten years. This is pure protection; there is no cash value to this policy, except the payment of the face value amount to the beneficiary that will occur upon your death.

If you do not have employer-sponsored life insurance, you'll need to provide your own. For a non-smoking young adult, the cost of $100,000, $500,000 or even $1,000,000 coverage is not very expensive. Term life insurance is a commodity, with very small differences between policies. Buy it from a low-cost company with a solid financial rating. Quotes are available online as noted above.

Disability Insurance
At your age, it is more likely that you might become disabled rather than die. For this reason, disability insurance is something to consider. The cost of disability insurance will be determined by the age, sex, and occupation of the applicant. For example, an office worker will pay less for this insurance than a construction worker. Quotes are available online as noted above

Car Insurance
This was discussed somewhat in Chapter Four, but there are two additional considerations:

Liability Limits
Your insurance policy has set limits as to how much the company will pay for various events. If you have some wealth, and you find yourself in a situation where a judgment against you exceeds your insurance coverage, a plaintiff can go after your wealth to recover the balance of the judgment. So, bear this in mind when setting policy limitations.

Setting Your Deductible
Understanding that insurance is a means of transferring your risk to an insurance company, you need to figure out how much risk you want to transfer. All of it? Some of it? This will determine what your insurance deductible will be.

The more risk you transfer, the more expensive the insurance will be. If you have a low deductible, say, $100, that means the insurance company will be responsible for any claim above that amount. If your deductible were $500, the insurance company is liable for $400 less, and your insurance premiums will be lower than with the $100 deductible. So, how low should your deductible be?

This depends upon how much risk you are willing to take. If you have an accident and have $4,000 worth of damage, and your deductible is $500, you will receive $3,500 from the insurance company. The question is, can you afford to pay $500 out-of-pocket to repair your car?

How Much Can You Handle Out-of-Pocket?

Here's where your Rainy Day/Capital Expense fund is useful. If you have several thousand dollars in this fund, you'll be able to handle the $500 deductible without too much trouble. If you have no reserve like the RD/CE fund, you might not be able to handle it.

So, if you are a reasonably careful and prudent driver, and are not "accident prone," and have some money in your RD/CE fund, I recommend that you have a deductible as high as you feel comfortable with. A figure of $500 will probably work. The lower insurance premiums will probably be worth it for you.

Health Insurance

Health costs in our country can be very expensive. If you have low income and no assets, you may be eligible for Medicaid. The threshold for eligibility for this program varies from state to state.

And of course, for those of any income who are 65 years old or over, Medicare is available. I suspect that most people reading this book will be eligible for neither Medicare nor Medicaid.

A National Problem

As I write, the issue of universal health insurance is a hot topic and a major concern for both political parties. Presently, health insurance for many people is often provided by employers and the two government programs mentioned above. Beyond those, people have to get their insurance through private insurance companies. Many people don't. There are an estimated 50 million citizens who are not covered by health insurance. They are vulnerable, and if you are one of these people, your assets, your wealth, and your health are all in jeopardy.

The Complexity of the System

Understand that medical care, insurance, and governmental and private responsibility are complex issues. The rates and fees set by the medical establishment, doctors, and hospitals assume that the costs will be borne by the insurance companies. How much they are actually paid by the insurance companies depends upon their arrangements with these companies.

Naked Is Not Good

If you are living your life without health insurance of any kind, you are said to be *going naked.* In the case of a medical need without insurance, hospitals are required by law to treat you in their emergency room. But, if you have assets, you may be charged for their services, and it ain't cheap. In fact, a good number of personal bankruptcies are the result of unpaid doctor or hospital bills. This is a situation you want to avoid.

Your Will

Everyone who has anything in the way of assets, such as a house, a car, a bank account, etc., needs to plan for his or her untimely death. What do you want to become of your assets? Who gets them? That's where a *will* comes in.

At this time in your life, when your finances are probably quite uncomplicated, a simple will would suffice. Formats, even software, for the development of a simple will are available at office supply stores such as Staples or Office Max. Or you can go online at **www.uslegalforms.com** or similar websites. Be sure that the form you use is specific to the state where you live. With the form in hand, probably the only decision you have to make is who gets what.

Dying "Intestate"

If you die without a will, known as dying *intestate*, the disposition of your assets will be determined by the courts. By the time the lawyers and accountants are done with your case, there may be very little left. Therefore, I strongly recommend that you have a will. Later in your life, when you have more assets and your finances are more complicated, your will should be drawn up by a lawyer experienced in estate planning.

Other Estate Planning Documents

Included in materials for the development of a will, there will be materials for the development of some other related documents you'll need.

A Durable Power of Attorney for Asset Management

This document will allow a person, designated by you, to act in your stead if you were to become physically or mentally incapacitated, and thus unable to handle your personal finances. Without such a document, the responsibility might very well go to someone who is not competent in this area. If this were the case, a local court might have to appoint someone to manage and/or administer your assets. You probably would like to make your own decision in this matter.

A Living Will

This is an important document that includes a durable power of attorney for health care. A living will allows you to state your wishes as to the desired medical treatment at the end of your life, in the event that you become terminally ill or injured, and are incapable of stating your desires for treatment (or lack thereof) at that time. You may state what you do, or do not, want done to you if you are unable to communicate. A durable power of attorney for health care can be set up to be "springing" – that is, to spring into operation at the time you become incapacitated.

The Importance of a Living Will

In the last couple of decades, two cases headlined in the national news showed the importance of a living will. Two young women, Karen Ann Quinlan and Terri Schiavo, were both in a persistent vegetative state and unable to tell their caregivers the level of care, if any, they wished to have. What should their families do? What would Karen or Terri have wanted? Should the quality of life determine the continuation of life?

These are deeply personal, moral, and religious issues that had dramatic effects on the young women involved and their families. Tragic as both cases were, many of the problems could have been avoided if they had created living wills. These two cases brought a national awareness to this issue. It's one that you should face as well.

Instructions for Your Survivors in Case of Your Death

This should be included in your will, but it would also be worthwhile to have a separate copy of these instructions given to one or more members of your family. These instructions should include what you want to be done with your "remains," as well as funeral arrangements, if any.

Guardianship for Minors

If you have minor children, you need to think through the issue of guardianship for them. The appointed guardian could be a family member, or perhaps a close and trusted friend. Sometimes, contemporary parents have a reciprocal arrangement whereby each set of parents agrees to take guardianship of the other's children in case of the demise of the children's parents.

CHAPTER ELEVEN
BUYING A HOUSE

For many people, the purchase of a home is the largest financial transaction of their lives. To own your home is the American dream, and most of us aspire to it. If you are careful, prudent, thoughtful, economically conservative, and have a bit of luck, you can do this. But it doesn't always work out when approached in a careless fashion.

In 2006, the housing industry began to have major problems. For the first time in many years, residential real estate prices entered a period of continuous decline. The financial instruments undergirding this market were not trading because their value could not be easily determined. This led to severe problems in the financial industry. Banks couldn't put a value on what they owned, and they stopped lending. The economy was grinding to a halt. Wall Street's problems were being felt on Main Street.

Home Ownership

One afternoon, I was listening to a radio broadcast of an interview with a young woman, probably in her twenties. It was disheartening to listen to her story. She and her husband (I'll call them Mike and Jody) had recently bought a home and expected to be living in their dream house. But their dream turned into a nightmare. What happened? There were three problems.

1. They bought at the top of the market. The house they purchased a few years ago for $350,000 was now worth $250,000.
2. When they bought the house, they did not consider that, in addition to the payment of principal and interest on the loan, they would have to make monthly payments for property taxes, insurance, utilities, and upkeep.

3. They financed their house with an 80% first mortgage and a 20% second mortgage.

They each got second jobs to make up for the financial short-fall in their income, but they would probably not earn enough money. There was a good chance that they would lose their home.

Stormy Weather

As I listened to this story, I was reminded of a book I read a few years before, *The Perfect Storm*. This true account told of three independent weather systems in the North Atlantic that came together in October 1991 to form a once-in-a-century meteorological event. There were 110-foot waves and winds of over 90 miles an hour. Many fishermen and women and many boats were lost in this occurrence. Meteorologists watching the radar screen called it "a perfect storm."

Mike and Jody bought their house in 2006, which was the beginning of a financial crisis so serious that it is referred to as a once-in-a-century event. Residential housing prices had appreciated dramatically in the preceding 15 years. Over-leveraged financial institutions held vast quantities of financial instruments whose values were inflated. Many of these were mortgage-backed securities reflecting an overpriced housing market, later called the housing bubble. Bubbles eventually burst, and this one was no exception. For Mike and Jody, in financial terms, just about everything that could go wrong did go wrong. The confluence of many factors, all working to their disadvantage, caused their "perfect storm."

Learn from Experience

First-time homebuyers can learn a great deal from the experiences of the young couple described above. There are many rewards for home ownership, such as:
- Putting down roots, belonging to a community, and having a place that is your own

- Owning an asset that usually appreciates over time
- Benefiting from being able to deduct mortgage interest and real estate taxes from income taxes
- Having an investment in real estate while using the investment as a place to live

But there are perils as well. In this chapter, I'll be looking at this couple's "perfect storm," and comment on the three problems they encountered. If you ever want to buy a house for yourself, this will be useful background for you. For illustrative purposes, I've added some plausible details to their story.

Problems to Avoid
Mike and Jody got themselves in deep water from the development of three problems.

Problem 1:Buying At the Top of the Market
To understand this problem, we need to understand some basic information, beginning with what markets are and how they work.

Markets
When a buyer and a seller meet and an exchange takes place, a market has been created. This happens for any item, including rare coins, cars, bonds, computers, gold, stocks, and houses. Generally, markets are cyclical. They go up and they go down. This means that a given item, like a rare coin, may be worth $3,000 at one time, $3,500 at another time, and $1,800 at yet another time.

But, what is the coin really worth? $3,000? $3,500? $1,800? More? Less? This question cannot really be answered. The value of any asset, including our rare coin, is the price that a perfect stranger would pay for it. There is really no such thing as an objective intrinsic value of an asset.

Let's limit our discussion to houses, particularly single-family residences.

There is a market for houses. People want to buy them and people want to sell them. If there are more buyers than sellers, the prices will go up. Conversely, if there are more sellers, the prices will go down. This is basic economics, supply and demand.

There are two aspects to the price you pay to buy a house: the particular house in mind, and the housing market in general.

The Particular House
At a given time, what should the house be selling for? You can make an estimate based upon what comparable houses in that neighborhood are selling for, or the per-foot cost of land and home construction in the area. This is not difficult to do, especially if you are working with a knowledgeable realtor.

The Housing Market
Where is the housing market at this time? What are prices like? Where have they been? These questions can be answered by doing some research on the Internet, or by talking to a trusted person knowledgeable in residential real estate.

Where are prices going? Is this a good time to buy a house at a decent price? Can you be sure of not overpaying? Are there real bargains out there now? These are more difficult questions to answer, and nobody can answer with certainty.

One factor to consider is the direction housing prices have been going in the last few years. Has there been a general rise in prices? Then perhaps prices will be going down. After all, markets do fluctuate. When prices rise very quickly however, the market often will correct itself (reverse its course), and the correction can be as fast or faster than its rise. That's the way markets generally work.

Mike and Jody bought their house after 15 years of rising prices. The market corrected itself, and prices fell dramatically. Their house, purchased for $350,000, was now worth $250,000 in the market. Will the value of their house ever get back to $350,000? Maybe. And given enough time, probably. The problem is whether they can hold onto it long enough for it to appreciate.

Now, two questions arise. Do they have the finances to sustain their ownership? What will it cost to own and live in this house? That leads us to their second problem.

Problem 2: Neglecting to Budget for Other Monthly Expenses

Mortgage loan payments typically include payment of principal and interest. Often, payments also include taxes and insurance on the house. If not, they have to be paid separately. Mike and Jody were paying $3,394 monthly for principal and interest. But taxes were $5,000 per year, and insurance was $2,000 per year. This total of an additional $7,000 means another $583 per month. Now, their total payment is $3,977. And that's just to own the house.

But they want to live in it, too. They need to add in the costs for gas, electricity, telephone service, cable TV, water/sewer, per-haps other utilities, and routine maintenance. This can easily add up to another $700 per month, which needs to be added to the $3,977 payment. Now they have to come up with $4,677 monthly, or $56,124 annually. If they can afford to own this house, they may not have any money left over on which to live. They are "house poor."

Problem 3: Financing With Two Mortgages

This kind of financing arrangement is very risky. When Mike and Jody bought this house, they put no money toward a down pay-ment, and thus had no equity in their house. Zero. It was totally, 100% financed. A responsible lender would not have allowed this arrangement to take place.

Understanding Mortgage Loans

A mortgage loan is a loan secured by a house that is used as collateral. Because the loan is secured, the interest charged on the loan is generally less than interest charged on unsecured loans, such as credit card charges. If the mortgage loan is not paid off, the house is subject to forfeiture.

Lenders (banks, thrift institutions, and credit unions) lend money with the expectation that they will receive interest for the duration of the loan, and will get back the principal amount loaned. If Mike and Jody were to have put 20% down, $70,000, on their $350,000 purchase price, they would have had some equity in their house. Then, if the price had fluctuated a bit and was less than they paid for it, they would still have some equity in the house and the lender would still have a valuable asset as collateral for the loan. As it was, the price decrease was so dramatic that their debt on their house is much more than its current value. They are "underwater," or "upside down," in this situation.

Loan Interest and Home Equity

If a lender is lending 80% or less of the house's value, it will probably lend for a lower interest rate than if the loan were for a larger percentage of the loan. In general, the more equity you have in the house, the lower the interest rate will be. Conversely, the less equity you have in the house, the higher the interest rate will be.

Mike and Jody took out a mortgage loan for 80% of the house's purchase price, but then took out another loan for the remaining 20%. They had no equity in the house and are now upside down.

How Could This Happen?

I wasn't there when the loan arrangements were made, but I suspect the scenario developed something like this.

1. Mike and Jody decided to buy a house for $350,000. They went to a mortgage broker to arrange financing. We'll call him Henry.
2. Henry told them they didn't need to have any money for a down payment. Financing of 100% of the house price could be arranged. A mortgage loan of 80% would be applied to $280,000 of the price. The initial interest rate was 7.5% for 30 years, and would be reset in two years. A second mortgage loan of 20% at a rate of 8.5% for five years would be applied to the remaining $70,000. This is sometimes call "80/20 financing."
3. Mike and Jody were hesitant about this arrangement. The first mortgage would require a monthly payment of $1,958, and the second mortgage a payment of $1,436, for a total payment of $3,394 per month. The payments for the year would total $37,344. They didn't think they could afford this.
4. Henry said something like, "Don't worry about it. After a few years, the house will appreciate 20% or so. You can sell it for $420,000, making a $70,000 profit, and then buy another house using the $70,000 as a down payment."
5. Mike and Jody really wanted to buy the house, but were skeptical about the financing. They asked, "What if house prices go down?"
6. Henry said, "Relax. Real estate values never go down. They only go up. Look what's happened in the last ten years. In this area, houses have appreciated by 12% every year." And so they might have. In some other areas of the country, residential real estate appreciated even more, and in some, less.

Why Would the Mortgage Broker Do This Deal?

The mortgage broker in this example, Henry, was unprofessional in his approach to making the loan, and took advantage of the naiveté of Mike and Jody. The loan never should have been made. Mike and Jody were unprepared financially, and didn't have a clear understanding of what they were getting into. There is a good chance that they will not be able to make the payments, and will thus forfeit the house. But, you ask, if they couldn't make the payments, and if the house were indeed fore-closed on, wouldn't Henry be on the hook for the default?

No. And that's the problem.

A Financial Crisis in the Making
Henry acted as an intermediary in this arrangement. He worked with the couple and sought to sell them a loan. Having done so, he sells the loan to another entity (we'll call it Institution A) and washes his hands of the loan. He collects his fee from Mike and Jody, and moves on to his next customer.

In the meantime, Institution A sells the loan to another business entity, Institution B. Now, Institution B assembles hundreds or thousands of loans, some poor ones like Mike and Jody's, and some of a better quality, and *securitizes* them. In this process, the loans are assembled into one big debt issue, and the indi-vidual debt instruments are then sold to someone else. The buy-ers might be other banks, or insurance companies, or a pension fund in Bolivia. Henry has been out of the picture for some time now.

After a while, some borrowers like Mike and Jody default on their loans by stopping payments of principal and interest, and forfeit their houses. Meanwhile, the holders of the debt instru-ments are not receiving the expected interest from them, and they lose their value. In fact, there are so many mortgage loans, of such varied quality, contained in the instruments, often nobody can figure out what they are worth. The holders of these securities would like to sell them, but since nobody can figure out what they are worth, no one wants to buy them. There is no market for them. They are stuck with them.

The unfortunate bondholders remind me of the last kids left in the children's games Musical Chairs and Hot Potato[1]. In Musical chairs, the last person still standing is the loser. In Hot Potato, the last person left has the beanbag. So, the bondholders have the bonds that nobody wants and are the last persons to have them.

In 2007-08, the preceding scenario, or something equally odious, happened many times. The securities based upon tens of thousands of mortgage loans of poor quality found themselves on the balance sheets of many banks, even some of the ones who did the securitization. The financial instruments might be CDOs (Collateralized Debt Obligations) or SIVs (Structured Investment Vehicles), or another type of debt. Because of their negative effect on the financial stability of the banks that owned them, the instruments were called "toxic assets." And thus began the worst financial crisis since the Great Depression.

There are lessons to be learned from this debacle. The story reveals how *not* to buy a house. But there is a right way to buy a house, and that leads to some ideas on how to do it.

How to Buy a House

Laws have been passed, and financial instruments and institutions have been developed, to make it relatively easy for many folks to purchase a home. But good sense and knowledge of basic economics has shown that not everyone can afford to own their own home. Yes, home ownership is the American dream, but not everyone can participate in the dream.

Should You Buy a House?

There are questions that you need to ask yourself.

1. Is your life settled enough that you can anticipate living in one place for at least five years? If you have the kind

---

1   In Hot Potato, children sit in a circle facing inward, a blindfolded caller is assigned, and a beanbag is put in play. The children toss the beanbag to another child as soon as they can, because they don't want to be stuck with it when the caller yells out "Hot Potato.

of job where you might be transferred every few years, it might not be worthwhile to buy a house. Even in a rising market, realtors' fees and closing costs can eat away at any profit you might make in only a few years of residency. And while you own the house, the real estate market may remain flat or decline, which would cause a loss on the house sale.

2. Can you afford it? Do you have enough money to buy it and live in it? Remember Mike and Jody's problems? How stable is your income? Is it on an upward trajectory? Do you have the time or expertise to make minor repairs or do decorating and landscaping yourself, rather than pay someone for these services?

3. Are mortgage loan rates affordable? In periods of significant inflation, such as the early 1980s, rates were as high as 15%. In 2004-05, they were down to about 5%.

4. Are there good houses or apartment rentals available which might be better for you? When you rent your home, you need not worry about the purchase cost or the upkeep of the structure. If you are transferred to another city, you won't have the hassle of having to sell your house. Also, you don't have to worry about the real estate market and whether you'll lose money on the sale of a house. And in some apartment rental complexes, there are often amenities like swimming pools and large party rooms, which you might not have in a house you own.

5. The question of whether to rent or buy a house is a complicated one. There are personal reasons as well as financial ramifications that need to be considered. Suze Orman has a thorough discussion of this issue on the Web at **http:/biz.yahoo.com/pfg/e10buyrent**.

Preparing to Buy a House
A decision to buy a house should come after you've assembled some cash by increasing your discretionary income using the suggestions in Chapters Four and Five of this book. You might

have budgeted specifically for a house purchase. You should have no significant debt to be paid, and your credit report should be good.

If, after reflection, you decide to buy a house, you have several more decisions to make.

- Decide on a price appropriate for your income level. A generally accepted rule of thumb is that your monthly mortgage payments (including taxes and insurance) should not exceed 25% of your gross income. For example, if your gross monthly income is $7,000, your monthly payments should be no more than $1,750.
- Figure out the net cost of your mortgage payment. For example, if your monthly payments are $1,750, this will total $21,000 for the year. Interest on the loan, and the real estate taxes you pay on the property, are deductible from your taxable income. So this will lower the net cost of the payment.

Here's how this works:

Let's say in a given year you earned $90,000 in income that is subject to income tax, and you are in the 30% marginal tax bracket. In your mortgage payments for the year, you paid $7,000 in interest and $3,000 in real estate taxes, for a total of $10,000. If you itemize your tax deductions, this means that this $10,000 is not subject to taxation. If it were, you would pay $3,000 in income taxes ($10,000 times 30%). Another way of saying this is, instead of paying income taxes on $90,000, you are paying the taxes on $80,000.

The $3,000 you saved on income taxes needs to be subtracted from the $10,000 you paid for interest and property taxes for the year. Thus, your net cost for interest and taxes is the $10,000 you paid minus the $3,000 you saved. Your net cost is $7,000. Table 11-1 shows this.

Table 11-1
Example of Tax Savings From Deducting Interest on Principal

	Interest on Loan	Property Tax	Total
Amount Paid	$7,000	$3,000	$10,000
Income Tax Savings	2,100	900	3,000
Net Amount Paid	$4,900	$2,100	$7,000

- Understand that your first house might not be your last house. The house of your dreams may not be within your grasp at this point in your life. Perhaps a "starter" house or a "fixer-upper" might be something you could afford now. In lieu of cash, do you have some talent that can be converted to "sweat equity," so as to increase the value of the house? After a while, when you have some decent financial equity in this house and when your household income grows, your dream house might be within your means.

- Decide where you want to live. With transportation costs being what they are, it makes sense to live near where you work. Do you have, or do you plan to have, children? If so, how are the schools in the area? Are there other young families with children with whom your kids can play? Look around the area's backyards for gym sets and outdoor toys. How's the shopping? Is the neighborhood stable? Drive around the area and get a feel for the community.

At this point, it would be worthwhile to see what's available to you by contacting a realtor. You might try **www.realtors.com** to search for someone appropriate. But remember that realtors generally work for the seller, not the buyer. Perhaps you can hire a realtor who would work for you.

Have Ready Cash

You'll need to garner some ready cash to buy a house. This will be needed at the time of the closing.

First, there's a down payment to consider. Try to have 20% of the purchase price to put down. You'll get a better interest rate with at least this much, although loans can be made with a lesser down payment. Also, with a smaller down payment, the lender may require you to take out mortgage insurance, another cost to you.

Then there are *closing costs* – attorney's fees, realtor commissions, processing fees, etc. These fees vary, but typically amount to 5-6% of the loan amount. Sometimes the seller can be persuaded to pay for some or all of the closing costs. This can be a consideration in the price negotiations you'll be involved in.

Some loan arrangements will include *points* (loan origination fees) that are calculated as one percent of the loan value. The interest rate on the mortgage is adjusted for having paid points. Payment of points can sometimes be negotiated, as can other closing costs.

If you're short on cash, I strongly recommend that you wait until your cash position is better before buying a house, and that you not take out a second mortgage or use credit cards for the additional cash needs. This can lead to real trouble later on.

Getting a Mortgage Loan

Let's assume that you have accumulated sufficient cash for a down payment and closing costs. You'll need financing for the remainder of the price. This will take the form of a mortgage loan, in which you pledge the property you bought as collateral for the money that must be repaid. Your lender might be your bank, credit union, savings and loan association, or local mortgage broker. You can go online with outfits like **www.lendingtree.com** and get rate quotes by e-mail.

When you approach a lender, you will need to provide some evidence that you can carry the loan (unlike Mike and Jody, described above). Bring last year's federal tax forms, bank statements, paycheck stubs, proof of other assets or income, and a list of your debts. This will be used to determine your creditworthiness. Based on this information, the lender will be able to give you an idea as to whether the loan will be available to you. This is sometimes called *preapproval* or *prequalification*.

A Word About Terminology

Strictly speaking, a *mortgage* is a document that secures a loan used for purchase of a property. A *mortgage loan* is a loan secured by a mortgage. Sometimes these two terms are used interchangeably. People talk about going to the bank to "get a mortgage," when actually they are giving the bank a mortgage, not getting it. This may seem picky, but you should keep the differences in mind so you can make sense of documents you may come in contact with.

The mortgage is the document and the mortgage loan is the money. You give the bank a mortgage and they give you a mortgage loan. You, the borrower, are the *mortgagor*. The bank, the lender, is the *mortgagee*. When a document states that the taxes are to be paid by the mortgagee, that means the bank has to pay it, not you.

Types of Loans

There are several variations in loan arrangements. These three are the most common:

Amortizing loan – This is the traditional, standard mortgage loan with a fixed rate. With these loans, you make equal monthly payments that are applied to 1) the principal (the amount borrowed), and 2) interest (the cost of borrowing the principal). Initially, most of the payment goes toward the interest, with a small amount reducing the principal. As time goes on and the principal is reduced each month, less of the payment has to go toward the interest and more can go to pay off the principal. This is the process of *amortization*. At the end of the loan duration, you have paid all the interest charges and the entire principal borrowed. Then, the mortgage is returned to you, at which time you're done with it. You own your home free and clear.

Non-amortizing (interest-free) loans – With this loan, you pay only the interest on the principal. None of your payment goes to pay down the principal. At the end of the loan duration, you still owe the entire principal amount. Your final payment is called a "balloon payment." All you've done is rent the loan money for that period of time. You've made no progress toward ownership.

Adjustable rate loans – These loans are often offered to naïve buyers. They have a low "teaser rate," such as 4.5% for the first three years. Then, the rate will be adjusted as the lender desires. I have never heard of an instance when the rate was lowered. A borrower can expect an increased rate – perhaps a substantial one – at the end of the three years. Jumps of 4% and 5% are not unheard of.

I recommend the standard, amortizing fixed rate loan. The only reason for getting either of the other loans is if you plan to live in the house for only a few years. In this case, however, I think it's better not to buy, but to rent a house or apartment instead.

Having selected the type of loan, there are two important aspects to be determined – the interest rate and the loan duration. These factors are separate, but related.

Interest Rates
Prevailing interest rates at any given time are primarily determined by the financial markets. Factors that influence these markets are the availability of funds, the present and anticipated inflation rates, and the actions of the Federal Reserve Bank. Rates can be ascertained online, or by referring to the financial section of a newspaper. The rate at which a lender will lend you money will be determined by the prevailing interest rates, your creditworthiness, and the duration of the loan.

Monthly Payments

Some monthly loan payment plans pay only P and I (principal and interest). You are then responsible for paying taxes and insurance premiums directly to the taxing agency or insurance company.

Other payment plans consist of payments for PITI (principal, interest, taxes, and insurance). In this case, the payments to cover taxes and insurance are accounted for by the lender separately from the principal and interest on the loan. The funds needed for taxes and insurance are held by the lender in escrow accounts, and disbursements are made directly from them to the taxing agency and the insurance company. At year's end, you'll receive a statement showing how much money went where.

Loan Duration

Fifteen and 30-year loans are most common, but many lenders will offer other loan durations as well. Interest rates on shorter durations tend to be lower than those of longer durations. This is because, from the lender's point of view, there is less risk in a shorter loan. For example, as I write, mortgage loan rates are 5.88% for a 15-year loan, and 6.22% for a 30-year loan.

Which is a better rate? Obviously, a rate of 5.88% is better than 6.22%. But the 5.88% applies to a 15-year loan. When the duration of a loan is shorter, the monthly payments are usually more, in spite of a lower rate. For example, consider a loan amount of $150,000 at these two interest rates.

As shown in Table 11-2, the 30-year loan interest rate is 0.34% more than that of the 15-year loan. Over the life of the loan, the total payments made on the 30-year are $105,354 more than on the 15-year loan. This reflects both the higher interest paid and the longer term of the loan.

Table 11-2
Payments on a $150,000 Loan (Principal and Interest)

Duration of Loan	Interest Rate	Monthly Payment	Total Payments Over Life of Loan
15 Years	5.88%	$1,256	$226,080
30 Years	6.22%	$921	$331,434
Difference	+.034%	-$335	+$105,354

The only positive factor favoring the 30-year loan is that the monthly payment is $335 less than for the payment for the 15-year loan. That's not much of a difference when you consider that the loan will be paid off in half the time with the 15-year loan. For this reason, I recommend that, if at all possible, you opt for a 15-year loan.

Other Interest Rates

For your easy reference, Table 11-3 shows the monthly payments for a $150,000 loan at several interest rates for 15- and 30-year durations. You can calculate monthly mortgage payments for varied durations, principals, and interest rates using the website **www.bankrate.com**.

Table 11-3
Monthly Payments for 15- and 30-Year Loans at Varied Interest Rates

Interest Rate	15 Year	30 Year
5%	$1,180	$805
6%	$1,226	$899
7%	$1,348	$998
8%	$1,433	$1,101

I encourage you to own your home, if appropriate and possible. It's usually an excellent long-term investment, as well as a great way to live. Buy a home you love and can afford. Enjoy your life living there.

INDEX

information can be obtained
ICGtesting.com
the USA
1953140415

9 780980 076929